Maria Jaoudi, Ph.D.

Christian Mysticism East and West

What the Masters Teach Us

PAULIST PRESS
New York / Mahwah, N.J.

The Publisher gratefully acknowledges use of the following materials: Selections from *The Vision of God* by Vladimir Lossky; copyright © 1983, St. Vladimir's Seminary Press, Crestwood, NY. Selections from *In the Light of Christ* by Basil Krivocheine; copyright © 1986, St. Vladimir's Seminary Press, Crestwood, NY. Selections from "The Mirabai Versions" in *The Soul Is Here for Its Own Joy,* edited by Robert Bly; copyright © 1996, Ecco Press. Selections from *We Are Three,* translated by Coleman Barks, copyright © 1987, Coleman Barks.

Cover design by Cynthia Dunne

Library of Congress Cataloging-in-Publication Data

Jaoudi, Maria.
    Christian mysticism East and West : what the masters teach us / Maria Jaoudi.
      p. cm.
    Includes bibliographical references and index.
    ISBN 0-8091-3823-9 (alk. paper)
    1. Mysticism. I. Title.
BL625.J26   1998
291.4'22—dc21   98-28247
                                                CIP

Published by Paulist Press
997 Macarthur Boulevard
Mahwah, New Jersey 07430

www.paulistpress.com

Printed and bound in the
United States of America

Contents

For Harry,
whose humor, lucid mind, and companion's
heart have inspired the ordinary and
extraordinary during our years together.

Acknowledgments

For the memory of my father, Ambassador Edmond A. Jaoudi, for our years in France, for his service in the French Resistance, for an abiding appreciation of the sacred pleasures that the French do so well: eating, painting, literature. *On ne peut pas oublier tous les* gold-pink sunrises over the undulating Mediterranean Sea.

To Reverend Lawrence Boadt at Paulist Press special thanks are due. Father Larry has been an untiring encourager and gracious editor through the ups and downs of creating chapter and book.

Introduction

Christianity, like Buddhism, has an abundance of denominations. Most people in the West, when asked about a Christian denomination, immediately think of either Roman Catholicism or a particular Protestant denomination, such as Episcopalian. This book attempts to elaborate on the spiritual aspects of a sometimes forgotten Christian tradition that contains within its label of Eastern Christianity a plethora of individual denominations both ancient and unique.

There are geographic and sociological reasons for the lack of awareness concerning the Eastern Christian denominations. For example, the Russian and Greek Orthodox communities were smaller than the earlier pilgrim churches in America; therefore, certain Eastern Christian branches became more insular. Like the Latinness of Roman Catholicism, the rituals, creeds, canons, belief systems, and indigenous ethnic languages that formed these Eastern Christian denominations, and the fact that these communities were now in America, did not change their basic beliefs and practices.

There are both theological similarities and differences between Eastern and Western Christian mystics. I have selected several personal favorites of mine to demonstrate the contemplative spirituality present among certain individual representatives: mystics who reflect the particular religious symbology of their tradition but who also have temperamental and artistic expressions with which I have resonated in my own spiritual growth and development over the years. Since there is an abundance of denominations in both East and West, I have remained with those traditions in which I have been personally involved in the hope that greater depth and understanding would be revealed through my own attractions and interests. Where spirituality is concerned, if one is not applying those truths and insights into one's own interior reflections and life, it is hardly spirituality or mysticism. As a professor I have humbly learned that my students respond to what they love. And a passion for the spiritual life, within a materialistic civilization that has so little awareness of the Spirit, must be called forth from the soulful depths of each seeker of God. Then one may discover the divine even in a shopping mall or a baseball game. One does, however, have to know *what* or *how* to reach that sacred center within so that that which is without may be responded to in a prayerful way.

As I will elaborate in Chapter 5, I was raised in the French Catholic tradition in Paris and Cannes, and in the Maronite tradition with some Melkite experiences in the Middle East. In the first chapters I focus on specific mystics as a way of bringing the reader into the experiences and the worldview of individuals who have their own tradition coursing through their veins and alive in their dreams and visions. In the last chapter I am much freer, more autobiographical, and broader in scope in the hope that this chapter on the arts and spirituality will enkindle a multimedia exposition on mysticism evoked through music, poetry, and painting.

Much of the text explores Hindu, Buddhist, Taoist, and Islamic Sufi as well as Christian sources. These traditions have also been a deep part of my life and profession. As a retreat director and professor of world religions, mysticism, and Asian studies, these four traditions have been the ones I have focused on over the years, from the profound metaphysics of the Hindu *Upanishads,* which were the favorite world scriptures of Joseph Campbell, the mythologist, to the further development of Sanskrit concepts and psychological truths in Buddhism, to the cultural metamorphoses and florescences of Buddhism as it moves from India into Tibet, China, Japan, and now the United States.

I am grateful that so much of my graduate study was on the differing forms of Buddhism, from the development of the Bodhisattva figure in China, she/he who compassionately enlightens other beings, to the healing integration of Tibetan tantric practice through meditation and visualization. In Japan the thriving grand aesthetics of art, architecture, and the martial arts blossom through the impact of the sixteenth-century Samurai. As the Dalai Lama of Tibet has observed, it should come as no surprise that Buddhism would flourish among the altruistic and democratic ideals of America, for the Buddha himself expounded such economic and political concepts.

Numerous college students have shared with me the importance of Taoism's emphases on harmonizing opposites through yin and yang within oneself, bringing this harmony into one's life commitments, and regarding and learning from the patterns in nature. As Thomas Merton described *Chuang Tzu,* one of the philosophical founders of Taoism, the role of freedom for the individual, and of humor as a necessary spiritual virtue for mental health, make Taoism relevant in accord with today's scientific and psychological discoveries.

What can one say of the Sufis but that they lead one to dance! They lead one to an ecstatic awareness of God that makes of the most ordinary experiences an encounter with wonder and music. Believe me, my friend, although I only provide a peppering of excerpts from Rumi and Kabir, they may open for you the door to the riches of Islam's mystical tradition.

Accordingly, I ask myself in writing this Introduction, what is my purpose in sharing the reflections of this book? I believe that these world mysticisms have helped me gain a deeper faith and opened me to the healing presence of the spirit alive in my own psychological workings and in the magnificent books of the human world and nature. The specific teachings of mysticism through spiritual writers, expressions through art and music, and the sacred that is evident in the smile of my five-year-old son waking to a new day of adventures are experiences that I have worked at appreciating more attentively through spiritual centering and mindfulness. I am grateful for the opportunities I have had to learn the language of mysticism. The language of mysticism is the Rosetta Stone needed to decipher the meaning behind the symbols and events of one's life.

Mysticism is placing God first by centering through prayer and meditation, by creating time and giving that time sacred space. Mysticism makes of the universe a mirror of what is already here in the "eternal now" of Meister Eckhart. It is the way of everyday life, of which Dogen the Zen Master writes, as here present for the looking and seeing through one's inner vision.

I hope that the reflections contained within this book will be a springboard to your own experiences and reflections in the arena of global mysticism and dialogue.

Personal growth according to world mysticisms affects the world from within, moving outward as consecrated action. Thus, the deeper one's contemplative life, the more profound becomes one's understanding of peoples, cultures, countries, and religions. As Paul Reps, the Zen Buddhist author, noted, "We all have the same color bones."

I

Finding the Center

The Christian West and East, though containing distinct emphases on methods of prayer, both focus on the ultimate goal of coming into God's presence and eventually entering the experience of union with God. In this chapter we focus on two methodologies from both Western and Eastern Christianity. These examples, however, by no means encompass the approximately two thousand years of Christian spiritual life.

The Cloud of Unknowing, an anonymous fourteenth-century English work, is not only an example of the highest mysticism of transcendence but also provides practical descriptions of how to begin to quiet the chatter of the mind, leading to the cloud of unknowing whereby one is joined to God.

Our focus in the Christian East in this chapter will be on *hesychasm,* which is a tradition of interior prayer, most notably the Jesus Prayer. We will not deal here with one particular component of the Jesus Prayer, but instead will attempt to present an outline of this helpful and magnificent tradition. The tradition is biblically based, stretching back to the early teachings of the Desert Fathers and Mothers, and the early and middle medieval theologians, and finally culminating in the now-famous Russian narrative, *The Way of the Pilgrim.*

The Author of *The Cloud*

William Johnston, one of the translators of *The Cloud of Unknowing,* describes the author as "a mystic, theologian, and a director of souls, who stands in the full stream of the Western spiritual tradition."[1] We can only conjecture about why the author of *The Cloud* kept his anonymity. Perhaps his motives had to do with a spiritual purity, acknowledging that he was called upon to share his wisdom but in no way to focus on his own personal identity. Jean Leclercq describes such a focus in religious literature as one that "belongs to the spirit.... It must be placed at God's service alone, not that of an author's reputation."[2]

Since the author's work is inbued with the thought of so many of his theological predecessors, such as Augustine, Bernard of Clairvaux, and Thomas Aquinas, he was obviously highly educated, and his writing bears the mark of someone who had thoughtfully discussed and dwelled on certain spiritual themes with his peers.[3] In any case, *The Cloud of Unknowing* is a timeless contemplative text that has tremendous appeal to modern searchers of the interior terrain. Its anonymity only adds to its spiritual beauty and effectiveness.

Leading to Love

For our anonymous author, love is the means and the end to entering the cloud of God's presence. The centrifugal force of all life and being is the Creator's ontological essence of love. God is "knowable" only through love:[4]

> Therefore I will leave on one side everything I can think, and choose for my love that thing which I cannot think! Why? Because [God] may well be loved, but not thought. By love [God] can be caught and held, but by thinking never.[5]

Love is able to grip us and draw us into a transcendent level of consciousness that is beyond our emotional attachments and troubles. In fact, love not only draws us into God's presence, but by coming into our true God-likeness through love, we will be able to approach our attachments and troubles with a new transformational perspective: "By the work of contemplative love [one] will be healed. Failing in this work [one] sinks deeper into sin further and further from God, but by persevering in it [one] gradually rises from sin and grows in divine intimacy."[6]

The Cloud of Unknowing contains a true contemplative understanding of sin. Sin is a failure to respond to one's own God-likeness. It further separates one from his or her true nature through the delusions of the mind. It is its emphasis on the consequences of *how* we think that makes *The Cloud's* definition of sin a contemplative one.

According to our author, we need not use elaborate theses or theologies about human nature. If we focus on growing in divine intimacy, we shall abandon the fabrications of the mind, the sinful and idolatrous pull away from our true nature, and come instead into the heart of divine likeness and presence.

The Buddhist Connection

Buddhism has three main schools: Theravada, Mahayana, and Vajrayana. These schools contain many denominations, just as in Christianity there exists denominations within Roman Catholicism, Eastern Christianity, and Protestantism. Within these schools denominations continually develop in both Buddhist and Christian history, for example, Methodism in Protestant Christianity and Zen in Mahayana Buddhism. Just as all three schools of Christianity believe in the teachings of Jesus in the New Testament as revealed truth, so also in Buddhism all three schools believe in the foundational teachings of the Buddha.

Buddha's first sermon after his enlightenment took place in Deer Park at Bodh Gaya in India. In this sermon he taught the Four Noble Truths and the Eight-Fold Path that every Buddhist, ancient or contemporary North American, practices.

The Eight-Fold Path and *The Cloud's* Definition of Sin

The Eight-Fold Path focuses on righteousness, the moral *dharma* of the universe. If we are to be in touch with our true Buddha-nature, we must do what is right. This is not an external morality, although it obviously includes social choices, but it is a morality beginning with contemplation and the mind. Right Contemplation and Right Thoughts are two of the path's approaches on how to come into contact with one's Buddha-nature. If I do not feel right or behave rightly, I am all wrong! I am not free but trapped in the wheel of wrongful thoughts, speech, and actions. Likewise, *The Cloud* states:

> Therefore, be attentive to time and the way you spend it. Nothing is more precious.... God gives only the present, moment by moment, for this is the law of the created order.[7]

Interestingly, although the word *dharma* can be translated in many ways, one of the most often used is *the law:* the law of righteousness.

I dwell on these two concepts of sin and righteousness only because today both words have negative connotations in the West that come from a representation based on external morality, not contemplative transformation. From a contemplative standpoint, sin is separation from one's divine Self, and righteousness is the way to remain centered in the divine through a unified body mind practice.

According to both *The Cloud* and basic Buddhism, there simply is no other way. In the words of *The Cloud:* "Keep in mind this general principle: if you possess God you will be free of sin and when you are free of sin you possess God."[8]

The Cloud of Forgetting

The author of *The Cloud* teaches us to enter the cloud of forgetting. This "cloud" is one whereby we may truly begin to enter God's presence because we are freeing ourselves from our ties to the ego. Only love, not thought, comes close to God, so we must enter that forgetting by letting go to allow God's immensity to emerge in our consciousness.

The first stage in prayer is discursive; that is, one must concentrate on spiritual texts and thoughts in order to learn to focus on healing, purifying, and transforming the mind from its usual chatter. Discursive prayer literally reorients the thought patterns. According to *The Cloud:*

> God's word, written or spoken, is like a mirror. Reason is your spiritual eye and conscience your spiritual reflection. And just as you use a mirror to detect a blemish in your physical appearance—and without a mirror or someone to tell you where the blemish is you would not discover it—so it is spiritually.[9]

Therefore, we make a conscious choice from being batted to and fro by arbitrary perceptions and emotions, to consciously choosing a focus of healing, love, and joy through texts and images that enrich body-mind-spirit development. We make a commitment to wholeness through God-likeness and thereby become open to the guidance of the Spirit. In the words of our author:

> For the act of remembering or thinking about what a thing is or does has a spiritual effect. Your soul's eye

concentrates upon it, just as the marksman fixes his
eye on his target. Let me say this: everything you think
about, all the time you think about it, is "above" you,
between you and God. And you are that much farther
from God if anything but God is in your mind.[10]

In order to enter the cloud of forgetting, we must learn to
forget those thought processes that separate us from our
true selves and enter the presence of God more clearly
reflected through the writings and imagery of people and
works that make a conscious effort to be closer to God's
nature and image.

Mary and Martha

The second stage of prayer for our author is contemplative surrender guided by love. No longer dominated by
busyness, fears, hostility, or the numerous variations of a
fragmented psyche separated from God's love, we begin to
open ourselves to the guidance of God's spirit through love.
According to the author of *The Cloud*, "the paragon of
such surrendering receptivity is Mary sitting before Jesus."[11]
Following the Christian tradition of his time, the author
conflates Mary of Bethany, sister of Martha, with Mary of
Magdala, but recognizes that this Mary "articulates the
right praxis of discipleship." For the purposes of our study,
we shall refer to Mary of Bethany simply as Mary in order to
preserve the spirit of *The Cloud's* intent while maintaining
the integrity of contemporary scholarship.[12]
The contemplative life is, according to *The Cloud*,
"Mary's part which shall never be taken away." The active life
is troubled and busy about many things, but the contemplative
life sits in peace with "the one thing necessary."[13] Mary's love
of Jesus gradually nourishes the seeds of wisdom within her
own Christ-like nature, leading to the third stage of prayer,

which is love discovering wisdom. By emptying oneself of the barriers in order to truly enter into Jesus' presence, Mary begins to grow the divine potentiality within her own person. In this way Mary becomes, through her love, another Christ. She will, by reason of her own transformation, become a preacher and vessel of God's spirit.

The Bodhisattva

The tradition of the Bodhisattva in Mahayana Buddhist tradition is similar to *The Cloud's* explanation of love discovering wisdom. The words *Bodhi Sattva* mean "enlightenment being." Depending on the culture and time, the Bodhisattva is either female or male. One of the most beautiful traditions is of China's Kuan Yin, about whom it is said: "She who hears the cries of the world."[14]

Mahayana has many distinguishing characteristics. Two of the most evident are the Bodhisattva-ideal and the relationship of the Bodhisattva's compassion to the experience of emptiness. In Mahayana Buddhism, *sunyata,* or emptiness, creates wisdom. Without the experience of emptiness we hook into the projections of our mind's ego patterns, and we cannot even come near to the enlightened state. Emptiness, expressed often in Chinese and Japanese art as the empty circle, is the pathway to wisdom. Yet it is not the final stage; returning to the world to embody the Bodhisattva's vow: "However innumerable sentient beings are, I vow: to save them all."[15]

The Buddha's last temptation was to not return to the world and teach. I often ask my students in our *Buddhism* course, "Why was it so difficult for the Buddha to come back?" In every class thus far, a student will inevitably answer: "Because the world is filled with pain, frustration, anger, and so forth. Why come back when you are in the bliss of nirvana?"

Buddhism's answer as to why the Buddha returns to the world mirrors *The Cloud's* image of Mary: because the experience of one's *true nature* makes of one's consciousness a fine balance of compassionate wisdom whereby one is compassionately in the world, but not of it. The wisdom embodied knows how much to go forth and how much to draw back. True contemplation brings emptiness into the world through compassion, but the contemplative must be able to discern when to draw back and reenergize spiritually. In the words of *The Cloud:* "So be very careful how you spend your time. There is nothing more precious. In the twinkling of an eye heaven may be won or lost."[16]

The Cloud of Unknowing

The cloud of unknowing is the experience in contemplation of God's presence when one has, through forgetting, banished "the countless distracting thoughts that plague our minds and restrain them beneath the *cloud of forgetting.*"[17] It is an experience of emptiness in which one does not even want to know where one is, who one is having dinner with, or what the latest news is. Before my friends who are reading this text jump to the conclusion that the author of *The Cloud* is unconcerned and uncompassionate about the world, I must state that quite the opposite is the case.

The author explicitly says, according to Clifton Wolters, that a person "becomes much more worth knowing when he is a contemplative...they become poised and cheerful, and able to mix with 'accustomed sinners' without being contaminated, and, indeed, attracting such to a godly life."[18] What is transformed ontologically then brings about change through action. However, the action is different because the person acting is imbued with the loving wisdom of the Holy Spirit.

We see a similar effect in the famous Zen poem:

> Before enlightenment
> I chopped wood and carried water.
>
> After enlightenment
> I chopped wood and carried water.[19]

So what happened? It is a change interiorly wrought, yet apparent in *how* I chop wood now and how I carry water now. For the author of *The Cloud,* "there are some who by grace are so sensitive spiritually and so at home with God in this grace of contemplation that they may have it when they like and under normal spiritual working conditions, whether they are sitting, walking, standing...."[20]

The ultimate aim of entering the cloud of unknowing is to be one with God. This oneness through forgetting helps one to completely re-enter the demands of life, not with the eyes of past ego patterns, but living spontaneously, creatively, through the freedom of the Holy Spirit. "A [person] cannot be fully active except he be partly contemplative, nor fully contemplative (at least on earth) without being partly active."[21]

In a section of her book, *The Wisdom of No Escape and the Path of Loving-Kindness,* Pema Chodron has a chapter entitled "Not Preferring Samsara or Nirvana." *Samsara* is the endless cycle of active *karma* in the world: all the suffering, injustice, and ignorance that never seems to end. *Nirvana* is the cessation of suffering, literally meaning "snuffing out," extinguishment. Chodron, as any true Buddhist would, describes how one may not prefer samsara to nirvana. She quotes Chogyam Trungpa Rinpoche:

> Hold the sadness and pain of samsara in your heart
> and at the same time the power and vision of the Great
> Eastern Sun. Then the warrior can make a proper cup
> of tea.

Chodron herself then comments:

> I was struck by it because when I read it I realized that
> I myself have some kind of preference for stillness. The
> notion of holding the sadness and pain of samsara in
> my heart rang true, but I realized I didn't do that; at
> best, I had a definite preference for the power and
> vision of the Great Eastern Sun. My reference point
> was always to be awake and to live fully, to remember
> the Great Eastern Sun—the quality of being continually
> awake. But what about holding the sadness and pain of
> samsara in my heart at the same time? The quotation
> really made an impression on me. It was completely
> true: If you can live with the sadness of life (what Rin-
> poche often called the tender heart or genuine heart
> of sadness), if you can be willing to feel fully and
> acknowledge continually your own sadness and the
> sadness of life, but at the same time not be drowned in
> it, because you also remember the vision and power of
> the Great Eastern Sun, you experience balance and
> completeness joining heaven and earth, but really they
> are already joined.

Please forgive me for such an extended quotation, for there
is still more worth quoting:

> There isn't any separation between samsara and nir-
> vana, between sadness and the pain of samsara and the
> vision and power of the Great Eastern Sun. One can
> hold them both in one's heart, which is actually the
> purpose of practice. As a result of that, one can make a
> proper cup of tea.[22]

Contemplation Gives Life Meaning

Pema Chodron well describes a perspective of "not preferring samsara or nirvana" that is only possible if one continually meditates and looks to one's own motivation and action. *The Cloud's* choice of Mary as an exemplar of the most authentic Christian person also points to the primacy of contemplation. Through contemplation one is able to live life fully, because one has emptied oneself of all the obstacles of the mind and entered the realm of one's God-likeness. Then and only then is one able to live, breathe, eat, make a cup of tea, and work in tune with the Spirit present in reality. To come into contact with the real means to let go, as Mary did, of all the busyness and demands and to take the time to truly enter the presence of God. When one returns to the activities of life after contemplation, God's presence is carried through the very pores of our body-emotions-mind.

In the Christian East the *way* one often is able to remain at the center with God through all the challenges of life is through the practice of the Jesus Prayer.

Hesychasm

The word *hesychasm* means quietude, stillness. The hesychastic tradition, which begins with biblical references to praying ceaselessly,[23] contains the early Christian emphasis on attaining a state of inner peace and stillness through centering on the name and presence of Jesus. It is believed that by focusing on the name of Jesus in conjunction with breathing in and breathing out, one begins to *become* the name through continual awareness. By entering the presence of God, ever focusing on God as a "secret occupation" of the mind and breath, one enters into God's presence, and therein one's thoughts, emotions, and actions become divinized. [24]

Whether in the tradition of Sinai, the monks on Mount Athos, or the Russian Jesus Prayer, all of the monasticism of the Christian East is founded on the interior prayer of the name of Jesus. This may be one reason the theological traditions of Eastern Christianity did not, for the most part, fall away from the reality of the incarnation as the bedrock of their spirituality. That the *Christos* became Jesus, the transcendent immanent, has affected all the developments theologically, including the conscious belief that we as humans may become divinized by coming to embody the presence of Christ.

> The Jesus Prayer is inseparable from the spiritual life of the Orthodox Church. It forms the nucleus of monastic life....
>
> We can ask what gives the prayer this universal value and what explains its historical longevity? What else but the name of Jesus which is the incandescent core of this prayer?[25]

Professor N. Cranic of the University of Bucharest goes on to describe more personally the effects of the Jesus Prayer: "I felt close to the spirit of nature, free from worldly tumult; I tasted the sweetness of the interior life and sensed the nearness of God."[26]

Mantric Prayer

Professor Cranic's words are mirrored as well in *The Cloud of Unknowing*, which points to the powerful results of mantric prayer, especially brief mental prayers interiorly spoken in conjunction with the breath. The author instructs the reader to "fix this word fast to your heart, so that it is always there come what may. It will be your shield and spear in peace and war alike."[27]

The Cloud recommends using one word, such as *God* or

love, to decondition and recondition the mind.[28] In the Jesus Prayer tradition of the Christian East, one word is also advised especially for the times when one is preoccupied by complex tasks and cannot afford to concentrate on a long sentence or phrase.

For our own purposes in discussing the value of interior prayer, it is up to the individual to find what best suits his or her needs and to acknowledge that those needs also change through the various passages of life. For example, a busy career person probably would find it difficult to concentrate on a phrase from scripture. However, one word, such as *love* or *Jesus,* may be more than enough to bring into awareness the reality of God's presence.

In the Christian East the most famous Jesus Prayer is "Lord Jesus Christ/Son of the Living God/Have mercy on me, a sinner." This prayer is more lengthy and was suitable, for example, for the Russian pilgrim in *The Way of the Pilgrim* who crossed harsh winter landscapes, aflame with the Jesus Prayer lighting up his thoughts and heart.

Today, however, along with the length of the traditional Jesus Prayer, are other theological considerations that many would find difficult. I will name two of these and then move on to other alternatives.

First is the obvious maleness of "Son of the Living God." The connotation that Jesus could only be born a son and on sonship as privileged status is a contradiction for women and men who are finally finding their voices as daughters and sons of God.

He *was* born male, but this was not necessary by essence. He is the one united to the *Word* of the Trinity, but not because he was male. Indeed, by grace he made all men and women children of God. Recently a T-shirt appeared, portraying the manger scene with one of the angels announcing "It's a girl!" The theological ramifications of that biological fact would be astounding, and to many welcome, in the face of the patriarchal suffering women and men have endured because of the underdevelopment of exactly what Jesus embodied "maternally": caring, healing, fecundly divinizing the ordinary, content in the domestic atmosphere of simplicity.

Jesus' maleness was certainly balanced and not patriarchally oppressive. Therefore, it would be ironic to fasten one's thoughts on sonship when being children of God was such an essential component of Christ-likeness.

The second linguistic problem is the phrase "Have mercy on me, a sinner." The doctrine of *penthos,* compunction for sins, is a mainstay of Eastern Christian piety. In the Catholic and Protestant West, remorse for one's sins is also a stepping-stone to purification. The problem with such remorse is that it can become the hub of one's being, one's self, one's identity. It is not healthy psychologically to continually state how sinful one is because that negative labeling does not release one into Christic transformation but instead bogs one down in identifying with a poor self-image.

The Jesus Prayer at its best is a linguistic and physical method using breathing to help enter a state of watchfulness: to be in God's presence, to enter into the reality of the sacred all around, to listen to the guidance of the Holy Spirit. If we know certain sociological and psychological truths now that the tradition was not aware of, we may look to improve the tradition without in any way losing the power of the name and the tender reality of Jesus still so timelessly transformative.

A Spirituality of the Heart

True centering prayer in the Eastern Christian tradition is grounded in the heart. The necessary detachment of attentive watchfulness is balanced by being aware of one's emotional state. Wisdom gained through detachment is harmonized by the compassion of the heart. The desired state of union with God attained by centering on the breath and on guarding one's thoughts is synchronized with an appreciation of our human nature as emotive beings.

It is our emotional dimension that keeps our spirituality alive, and the awareness of the preciousness of life is maintained by being fully engaged in life's activities. What the Jesus Prayer tradition offers us is a wonderful home of awareness that we carry within us, no matter the external situation.

> A heart that has been completely emptied of mental images gives birth to divine, mysterious intellections that sport within it like fish and dolphins in a calm sea. The sea is fanned by a soft wind, the heart's depth by the Holy Spirit.[29]

By continually practicing the Jesus Prayer, one is able to discern more and more fully, through the Holy Spirit, when to act, how to act, what to say, and often more importantly, what not to say!

When our interior being is transformed and we come to abide in God's presence, our emotions change as well, becoming "sweet"[30] and less prone to knee-jerk reactions. Mere emotional reactions have the capability to engulf us in their virulence of anger, hatred, and judgmental narrow-mindedness. Indeed, we often become so attached to our emotional blocks that the reaction itself becomes reality to us. Here is where the wisdom of detachment, guarding one's thoughts, and spiritual warfare become obvious. If strong, violent emotions are internally identified, we can halt them at the gate of our hearts, dismantle them, and choose to comprehend the why of our reaction. Herein lies freedom from our own reactions and a new grounding in transformative calm. "Once the soul starts to feel its own good health, the images in its dreams are also calm"[31] because we have come home to our true sacred self-image. We come closer and closer to our identity inasmuch as we are aware of God's being present on every perceptual, sensorial, and emotional level. Within our dreams, happenings, and relationships the Spirit is guiding us, and now, due to our continual centeredness through the Jesus Prayer, we are able to listen and follow the Spirit.

It should be noted that a focus on the heart as primary is not unique to the Eastern Christian tradition. In most of the spirituality of the Western Christian tradition, devotional love was and is most often recommended as the basis of solid spiritual practice. From Augustine, who said he would only write theology "with a flame in his heart,"[32] to Karl Rahner and his intense piety of the Sacred Heart, we see that most of the great mystical theologians do not separate the heart and the intellect.

The *Bhagavad Gita,* one of Hinduism's most sacred texts, states that *bhakti* yoga, the way of devotional love, is actually more important than *jnana* yoga, the path of intellectual insight. Even Gandhi, who recited the entire *Gita* as an integral part of his continuing prayer practice, declared: "Above all else, I am a bhakti yogi."[33] This surprises many people, since most would think that a person of Gandhi's social accomplishments would have been dedicated to the third path in the *Gita, karma* yoga, the way of social action and work, which would be what most would think that a person of Gandhi's social accomplishments would have been dedicated to. However, for Gandhi, as for Augustine, Rahner, and the hesychastic tradition, it is devotional love that keeps their vision alive. The way of knowledge and the way of social action would dry up without the live coals of devotional love. Henri Nouwen once asked Mother Teresa how she could do so much. She replied that she never neglected her own prayer life. Without her prayer life, she could not

have given so much of herself because God's love was her
energizer and ongoing inspiration.

In the Christian East, it is acknowledged that theology
cannot exist in practice without focusing on the incarna-
tional reality of Christ alive within us. Hesychasm has been
practiced by both simple and sophisticated people in order
to remain affectively aware of God's presence: "It is no
longer I who live, but Christ who lives in me!" (Gal. 2:20).

Balance

Whether it is Mary as the symbol of the contemplative
life in *The Cloud of Unknowing,* the Jesus Prayer in hesychasm drawing us inward, Buddhist meditation, or Hinduism's *bhakti* yoga, the contemplative emphasis on
remaining centered is primary. All these traditions speak of
the importance of remaining fundamentally connected to
God at the center. The very word *yoga,* for example, means
to be "yoked" to God. Therefore, *bhakti* yoga yokes one
totally to the One reality that permeates all our inner and
outer worlds, God present in all life.

The goal of all these traditions' emphases on contemplation is to remain aware of the reality of our oneness with
God. Once one is centered, there are other paths that may
better suit us physiologically and temperamentally. The key
is a balanced spiritual perspective focused on returning to
the center from which love, wisdom, and power flow.

Hinduism's three paths of *bhakti, karma,* and *jnana*
yoga give the world the gift of balance. No path is best in
itself, according to the *Gita,* since each path may lead to
imbalanced extremes. Even too much *bhakti* may lead to
blind faith in authority, whether in the form of unquestion-
ing adoration of a guru or adherence to an institution's
dogma. The follower should also be encouraged to integrate

jnana, deeper intellectual insights, to understand his or her own motives and mind and thereby maintain a healthy skepticism in *bhakti* practice. *Karma* yoga might also be prescribed as a path of practicing through one's action and work all that love experienced in prayer.

Each of us, then, would come to empathize with and understand our own needs and imbalances. It should therefore be a simple task to move into areas where we need more balance to grow into whole and holy people.

The great medieval paradigm of Western and Eastern Christianity is still appealing and practical today: to bring one's prayer into life, the life of the mind, one's heart-life, our daily activities with family, work, and community. Contemplation gives us the detachment and self-love to really live well, a worthy goal that is accessible to each of us.

God Is My Partner: A Practical Application

We can practice mantric prayer and watchfulness during our ordinary daily activities, deepening our awareness of life moment by moment and transforming our minds through an affirmative word or phrase. Most spiritual traditions acknowledge that the adult mind needs to be re-educated. Whatever our usual thought foci, most of us could benefit enormously from a new perspective. We can begin our mental training by establishing thoughts that are focused on God devotionally and on transforming our lifestyle patterns.

When I was pregnant with my son, I had gestational diabetes, and there were possibly tremendous risks to the developing fetus if my insulin level increased. In addition to drastically controlling my diet, having my blood-sugar level checked weekly, and exercising by swimming, I would breathe in the prayer "God is my partner" and breathe out the affirmation "Baby is well." I repeated this prayerful affirmation continuously, while swimming, waiting for appointments with students, driving, any time an opportunity presented me with a few spare minutes. The serenity, the quiet confidence that filled me with God's care, was remarkable. Not that I was not worried: my first words as my son entered the world after twenty-three hours of intense labor were "Is he normal?" However, the major focus of the pregnancy was positive rather than negative (dwelling on the fear of possible birth defects). Harrison is a healthy, intelligent, happy child; and I am delighted that more energy was spent on affirming his being than on possibilities that never materialized.

I still use that prayer, substituting different words or ideas depending on life's circumstances. These phrases work well for me, but someday I may want to create or repeat another phrase that might have more significance for a particular situation.

Centering our thoughts on a mantric phrase creates in us a deeper devotion to the sacred self. It makes us more aware, more watchful, because we are not rehashing fears, worries, or other negative thought patterns. God, then, is truly able to be our partner. God is with us more profoundly in our thoughts, and we direct our lives more harmoniously through the guidance of the Spirit.

II

Becoming Whole: Finding Light, Discovering Peace

According to the Taoist tradition, wholeness is the mirroring within ourselves of the complementarity of opposites in the laws of the cosmos. These polar forces of yin and yang are present in how the body maintains balanced health through, for example, the application of Chinese medicine, and in all the systems of life on the planet. The beauty of the Taoist tradition is that yin and yang may be applied to many aspects of one's life, relationships, and world.

Being whole means finding one's center and remaining there as the basis of spiritual growth. In this chapter we will study Symeon the New Theologian in the Eastern Christian tradition, and Catherine of Siena in the Western tradition in order to see specifically how the steps toward wholeness are described by these two medieval saints.

Wholeness is never complete. The very nature of living the spiritual life is to learn when one needs to push and when one needs to listen and appreciate those pauses in life that imbue our perspectives with meaning.

Catherine and Symeon are very different people coming from dissimilar cultures. Yet we will find remarkable similarities in their explanations of spiritual transformation.

Symeon the New Theologian

Symeon is called the New Theologian because he revitalized Eastern Christian theology. Like Francis of Assisi in the thirteenth-century Christian West, Symeon in eleventh-century Greece, through his own prayer experiences, came to transform the tradition of his day with the insights of his experiential theology. As John Meyendorff states,

> "The Byzantine Church canonized Symeon the New Theologian, and generations of Eastern Christians have seen in him the greatest mystic of the Middle Ages. By so doing, Byzantine Christianity has recognized that, in the Church, the Spirit alone is the ultimate criterion of truth and the only final authority."[1]

The Gift of Tears

One of my reasons for choosing to focus on Symeon and Catherine in this chapter on wholeness is the emphasis of both of them on the gift of tears. Both saints speak to us in great detail concerning a gift that we moderns have forgotten can be spiritually edifying, but to which so much psychotherapy is directed. Tears are healing, and these two saints speak of tears as a gift because their occurrence is often unexpected and sometimes overwhelming. In Symeon's own words, "Tears flood and wash out the house of the soul; they moisten and refresh the soul that has been possessed and enflamed by the unapproachable fire."[2]

Symeon's description of tears has a long history, tracing its roots into both Testaments and into the Eastern theologians who preceded him. The Hebrew scriptures, especially the Psalms, emphasize the purgation of tears and the joy arising out of lamentation:

> O Lord my God, I cried to Thee for help, and thou hast
>   healed me.
>
> Thou has turned for me my mourning into dancing;
> thou hast loosed my sack cloth
> and girded me with gladness.
> That my soul may praise Thee and not be silent.
> O Lord my God, I will give thanks to thee forever. (Ps 30:2,
> 11-12)[3]

In the New Testament Jesus himself weeps, and those who demonstrate their devotional love and commitment through tears are considered more sincere in their *metanoia,* conversion.[4]

Some of Symeon's most important and earliest influences include primarily Isaac the Syrian, who rivals even Symeon with his poetic and single-minded emphasis on tears:

> If we arrive at stillness, we shall be constant in weeping.
> For this reason we should beseech our Lord with an
> unrelenting mind to give us this. If we receive this gift—a
> gift which surpasses all others—then through weeping
> we shall enter purity; and when we have entered there, it
> will not be taken away from us again; right up to the day
> of our departure from the world. Blessed, therefore, are
> the pure in heart who at all times enjoy this delight of
> tears and through it see our Lord continually.[5]

Macarius, Evagrius Ponticus, Ephrem the Syrian, John Chrysostom, John Climacus, John Damascene, Theodore the Studite, and Gregory of Nyssa are also influential writers of the Christian East who dwelt extensively on the healing benefit of tears. They believed one attained a complete internal purity, manifested as tears leading to the freedom experienced through divine union. John Climacus, for example, states, "The person wearing blessed God-given mourning like a wedding garment gets to know the spiritual laughter of the soul."[6]

For Symeon the gift of tears is intrinsic to spiritual growth as a spiritualizing baptism initiating the unfolding process. Symeon, then, assigns tears a potent role throughout the spiritual journey. He is, as mentioned, the inheritor of the biblical tradition in which tears are a continuous witness emphasizing a person's sincerity and ongoing development in curative well-being. Psalm 42, for instance, presents a prime model of tears as a physiological symbol of coming home to God and to one's own true self:

> As a deer yearns
> for running streams,
> So I yearn
> for you, my God.
>
> I thirst for God,
> the living God;
> when shall I go to see
> the face of God?
>
> I have no food but tears
> day and night,
> as all day long I am taunted,
> "where is your God?"
>
> This I remember
> As I pour out my heart,
> how I used to pass under the roof
> of the Most High. (Ps 42:1-4)
>
> Send out your light and your truth;
> they shall be my guide,
> to lead me to your holy mountain
> to the place where you dwell. (Ps 43:3)[7]

These lines explain the passage from conversion to hunger for the continuous awareness of God's presence. Now a home is desired for God within, a place where one's innermost self may dwell (Psalm 43:3). The imagery of home will be pivotal in Symeon's Christ-centered theology of indwelling, the shaping of the self into the image and likeness of God, the most profound contemplative resting within the interior mountain of healing and transfiguration:

> If God brings you to the mountain, climb it with eagerness, for I know well that you will enjoy the vision of Christ transfigured and shining more brightly than the sun with the light of the Godhead.[8]

This is why those who mourn in the Beatitudes are blessed and shall be comforted (Mt 5:4). They are mourning, grieving, weeping for a state of reality that calls them to end their homesickness and enter the kingdom of God that is already here once we become conscious of God's ever-abiding presence.

Symeon the Theologian of Light

The purification of one's consciousness leads one into that awareness of God's consciousness which is often manifested, for Symeon, as an experience of the light of Christ.

Symeon the New Theologian and the fourteenth-century Gregory Palamas in his *Defense of the Hesychastic Saints (The Triads)* are sequential mystical theologians glorifying the radiance of God in the Eastern Christian illuminative tradition. God's transcendence is frequently described as ecstatic light.

> It is clear that Symeon stands for the basic understanding of Christianity as personal communion with, and vision of God, a position he shares with hesychasm and with the patristic tradition as a whole.[9]

Symeon never tires of the metaphor of light: light is the Christ-reality, the manifestation in the created realm of the infinite One made incarnate. As Vladimir Lossky states in his book, *The Vision of God:*

> Saint Symeon considers the same reality, only on the level of pneumatology. For him it involves above all a revelation of the Holy Spirit in us, the life in grace which cannot remain hidden but manifests itself, on the higher plain of eternal life, as light.[10]

Symeon's vision is both personally and soteriologically relevant to a contemporary theology encompassing the earth and the entire cosmos: "The light encompasses all the manifestations of God."[11] In this category, the integration of the human body is also essential to a theology expressing the immanent dimension of the invisible become visible:

> Imagine now that the body is a palace and that the soul of each of us is a royal treasure. God, who is joined to the soul thanks to the observance of the commandments, fills her entirely with divine light and transforms her into god as a result of God's union, God's grace.[12]

Symeon's work is important because we can apply his unitive insights into a balanced theology of the eternal kingdom present here and now. In Symeon's words:

> Perfectly united to God, are those who have wholly possessed Christ in themselves by action and experience, by perception, knowledge, and contemplation.[13]

Therefore, light is the transcendent God visibly perceived in the pursuit of wholeness:

> It supplies perfect discernment, and by itself is a good guide to those who follow the spiritual sea [cf. Wisdom 10:18]. It is this that I pray may be granted you by God, and especially now, that you may discern your affairs in a manner pleasing to God and may so act and endeavor

> that you may find Christ, as Christ even now cooper-
> ates with you, and in the time to come will bestow on
> you abundantly the enjoyment of the illumination that
> comes from God.[14]

Light preceded most of Symeon's intense stages on the
ascent of the spiritual ladder. As Symeon climbed into the
deepest center of the indwelling divine within, his light mysticism became wholistically unitive. This signifies that the
health of the spirit on the spirit/psyche levels will eventually affect the material levels as well. As the light bathes the
self in divine radiance, one's psyche is transformed,
divinized, until finally the body also becomes a true temple
of the sacred self:

> To say that the One who is truly God takes form in us
> means that Christ assuredly transforms us, recreates
> us, and changes us into the image of the Godhead. So
> that the one who has acquired a good heart as a result
> of toil and practice of the commandments becomes
> the dwelling place of the entire Godhead who is the
> extremely good treasure.[15]

Symeon is therefore through light bridging the invisible
and the visible into one Christ-centered kingdom. In the
words of Krivocheine:

> The fact that humans,[16] inhabiting the world, can have
> within the One who is outside of all space and upholds
> the cosmos by divine strength fills Symeon with admi-
> ration: "O the immensity of ineffable glory, excessive
> love! The One who contains all, lives inside a mortal,
> corruptible being. All things are in the power of the
> One who dwells in humans; indeed, a human becomes
> like a woman carrying a child. Amazing, wonder of an
> incomprehensible God. Works, mysteries, defying com-
> prehension! A person knowingly carries God within as
> light, the One who made and created everything,

including the one who bears God. This one bears God
within like a treasure transcending words, utterances,
quality, quantity, image, matter and figure, shaped as
God is in ineffable beauty, altogether simple as light."[17]

Light is the center of the universe in the mystical vision of
Symeon. Perhaps as C. G. Jung understood, light symbolizes
attracting love, the complementary aspects of oneself being
drawn into union. The illuminative stage is also the transformative stage. According to Jungian psychology, this
ongoing process of growth continues even in our mature
years, sometimes experienced as an enlivening attraction
toward those weak areas in our own self that need to grow
and stretch. Very much influenced by the Taoist yin and
yang, which we will investigate later in this chapter, Jung
labeled these two forces *anima* and *animus,* very much influenced by the Taoist yin and yang, which we will investigate
later in this chapter. Suffice it to say, Symeon is attracted to
God, to soul development; his spiritual ascent is numinous.

In his psychological works Jung describes numinous
"hooks," whether they be religious, in the form of a person, or
an idea, or a goal, or even a place that is glowing, luminous
with meaning for us. We long for this place; we hope to possess this person or place or idea until it becomes integrated
within our being as a dimension of our own personality development. What Symeon experienced as light was what he
needed to experience in order to become whole. It was the
light that channeled the enormous power and energy of his
human *eros* and changed it into the gentle and giving compassion he so ardently expressed in the religious community on
Saint Marines that he established in his later years. His kind-
ness to the women, men, and children who came to the island
from all walks of life became legendary. He walked with a staff
like the good shepherd he was, serenely giving counsel, helping people who came to see him from every direction.

Light Deepening Into Awareness

Following initial conversion, in the quieting of spiritual advancement and in that homecoming of rest in the depths of experiencing God's transformative healing, light deepens into awareness. Light as awareness of divine presence creates a radiant love, healing one's internal divisions and wounds and eventually helping one to become that sacred presence that one has begun to be conscious of at the core of one's being.

The medium of light is a key to Christian resurrection. The light of Tabor, the resurrectional glorification of Jesus in spirit and body, is now reborn through initial conversion to actualized centeredness:

> The light which the apostles saw on Mount Tabor...was the light belonging by nature to God: eternal, infinite, uncircumscribed in time and space, existing outside created being....

> At the time of the Incarnation the divine light was as it were concentrated in the God-Human, in whom divinity dwelt bodily....It was this light of the divinity, the glory belonging to Christ by virtue of his divine nature, which the apostles were able to contemplate at the moment of transfiguration. The God-Human underwent no change whatsoever on Mount Tabor, but for the apostles this was a departure out of time and space, a glimpse of the eternal realities.[18]

What the integration of the God-Human signifies is a total remaking of the person on the level of the body, psyche, emotions, and spirit. The New Testament baptism in the spirit is the initial, committed step, the *metanoia* turning one's perspective toward God on all levels of the self (including the physical). Living in the light existentially remakes and molds the self into the image and likeness of God.

In this *Thanksgiving*, Symeon speaks of a certain epiphany of the unknown, indescribable God in the soul of those who struggle for salvation. One might call this a "localising" of the infinite, formless Godhead. Symeon, who did not suspect such a manifestation might be possible, was filled with amazement. Not only is God seen, but we are incorporated into God. "Whence, in what manner could I have learned that anyone who believes in you becomes incorporated in You, and reflects this Godhead? Who will believe this?—This one becomes blessed, having become a blessed member of the blessed Godhead." Symeon then sees God inside him: "Wondrous! I see in me the One who I believed to be in heaven, I mean you, O Christ, my Creator, my King."[19]

Light, then, is the medium of the invisible spirit revealing the love of God through presence:

> Those who are worthy, those who are united with God, may come even in this life to a vision of "The Kingdom of God coming in power," as did the disciples on Mount Tabor.[20]

It is a real experience, yet paradoxically not totally in the material realm, although mysteriously viewed therein. Symeon, as a partial Neoplatonist, describes the light as an intellectual vision transcending any description. Nevertheless, just as at Tabor, Symeon does see the resurrectional Christ: luminous, brilliant, splendorous. In Symeon's own words:

> Being enlightened by the divine light changes us completely. It gives us divine awareness: indeed, whose mind, soul, and heart would not be changed after seeing You, after being enlightened sensibly by your glory, your divine light? Who would not obtain the extraordinary gift of seeing, of hearing in a different manner, O

> Saviour? For the mind is immersed by Your light. It
> becomes effulgent and is changed into light. It
> becomes similar to Your glory, and it is called Your
> mind. The one chosen to arrive at such a state deserves
> to possess Your mind, for this one becomes insepara-
> bly one with You.[21]

For Symeon, however, the medium of light is never a reality
to which we may become attached as such. This would be
idolatry, and one can easily detect here the spiritual truth
behind Islam's unwillingness to depict the divine through
representational art. Symeon does, however, respectfully
believe in the incarnation, so that light is acceptable as a
revelation of presence:

> But you, O light, shine upon them, shine that in seeing
> you they truly believe that You are the true light and
> that You will make like Yourself the ones to whom You
> are united as light.[22]

God is revealed as light embodying love and consciousness
of the sacred. Light may draw us, but it is love and consciousness that deify us and help us to become whole. In
Symeon's inimitable words:

> So may we make our dwelling in God, as we live with
> the ineffable light in the imperishable life, in the joy
> unspeakable, in the unutterable glory and brightness
> that is seen...and adored forever. Amen.[23]

Christ Is the Light of the World

The light that redeems Symeon is Christ, the light that
reveals the mysteries of the cosmos. God is the light of the
universe, and our home is the immortal center and foundation of the theological meaning of light: the implications of

light as the illuminative path revealing the heart of Jesus as devotional love.

We spoke of devotional love in the previous chapter as that love found in human love as clearly as such relationality is found and discovered in the God-relationship. The devotion to the Other explains to the one experiencing such a "going-toward" the expansiveness of his or her own capability and potentiality to love.

Pema Chodron, in her Buddhist reflections in *Start Where You Are: A Guide to Compassionate Living,* describes this "going-toward" rather than struggling against others in our relationships:

> It all starts with loving-kindness for oneself, which in turn becomes loving-kindness for others. As the barriers come down around our hearts, we are less afraid of other people. We are more able to hear what is being said, see what is in front of our eyes, and work in accord with what happens rather than struggle against it.[24]

In the illuminative stage, then, love is equated with light, with all reality glowing, with this seeing with new eyes what is before and around us. This new vision is still present in the ultimate stages of union with God, but one is more quieted, more at home with the Beloved, so that the spark gradually becomes a continuous awareness rather than the sudden shocking aspect of new infatuated love.

In the Judeo-Christian tradition, the First Commandment describes total devotional love of God on all levels of internal and external existence as the steady criterion of faith and spiritual growth: the way of love expressing complete trust in the Beloved. Whether in the mysticism of the *Song of Songs* or in Symeon's ecstatic *Hymns,* the love of the Beloved is the call that the mystic answers on the level of devotion: "O my God, that I may always glorify You and sing Your power in unending hymns forever and forever. Amen."[25]

The spiritual secret Symeon discovers and that fills his being with light and love is God's own commitment to Symeon:

> Receive of the love for my divine realities in your heart, eternal blessedness which I by my Incarnation have prepared for you as for a friend, so that you might always be my banquet partner ineffably at the table of my kingdom, of my heaven with all the saints.[26]

The secret is that "we ourselves shine brightly and meet the Bridegroom at the resurrection of his brightness and enter with God into the kingdom of heaven (Mt. 25:10) and enjoy eternal benefits."[27]

For Symeon, following the traditional Christian symbolism of the mystical marriage, Christ is the light and the Bridegroom. The metaphor of marriage also unites the anima and animus, joining within one's soul the complementarity of opposites. In Symeon's mysticism of light and union, this integral wholeness of the self is particularly experiential:

> "God is light" says St. Symeon, "and God communicates this brightness to those who are united with God, to the extent that they are purified. Then the extinguished light of the soul, i.e., the darkened spirit, knows that it is rekindled, because the divine fire has embraced it. O miracle! The Human is united to God spiritually and corporally, for one's soul is in no way separated from the spirit, nor the body from the soul. God enters into union with the whole person."[28]

"God enters into union with the whole person." Symeon is thus solidly in the tradition of Moses, Jesus, and the early and medieval saints of Christianity who elaborate on the epiphany of wholeness for the Christian as the vision of the light of Tabor.

The vision of Mount Sinai finds its fulfillment, its plenitude realized at last on Mount Tabor, where Moses and Elijah (who had also, like him, received a figurative vision of God) appeared on either side of the transfigured Christ....The theme of Christ's transfiguration reappears constantly in the writings of the Byzantine theologians; it will be the nucleus of their doctrines on the vision of God.[29]

The Light of Tabor

The light of Tabor is associated in the Eastern Christian tradition with Jesus' transfiguration on Mount Tabor. Mystics from other traditions, as well as from Western Christianity, may not focus on Tabor but will nevertheless draw on other scriptural references of light in the Old and New Testaments, or in the scriptures of, for example, Hinduism: the *Vedas, Upanishads,* and the *Bhagavad Gita.*

Light has always played an important role in the consciousness of humankind, both as symbol and reality. Light, once worshipped as sun-divinity, evolves into the light shining invisibly within. Krivocheine quotes Symeon:

> Thus at the setting of the sensible sun comes the sweet light of the knowable star, certifying in advance and guaranteeing the light without end which must succeed it.
>
> Symeon therefore distinguishes the light of the vision from the light of the sun, but also from the light "that does not set," of which it is nevertheless a guarantee.[30]

Symeon's light is indwelling; it is the light that makes one conscious and symbolizes that consciousness. It is known and symbolizes consciousness because of the great gift of discerning clarity that accompanies experiences of light:

> It rises within my poor heart like the sun, the solar
> disk. It appears round, indeed luminous, like a flame.
> The entire soul is transformed by divine clarity.[31]

Internal Clarity

For Symeon, coming closer and closer to consciousness of self through ongoing healing and transformation
has to do with the clarity we develop through our prayer
life, which is then enacted in our daily lives: "It is, after all,
the lamp of the soul, that is to say, insight, which comes to
know the divine fire."[32]

According to Evelyn Underhill in her timeless classic,
Mysticism, "All conversion entails the abrupt or gradual
emergence of intuitions from below the field of consciousness, an alteration in the self's attitude to the world."[33]
These intuitions, formed by consciousness, are in fact the
very nature of deepened awareness.

The more conscious we become, the deeper our
insights are, the wiser we become. We gain a knowledge that
transcends the intellect, yet represents an integrated intelligence correlated with wisdom. Thomas Spidlik, in *The Spirituality of the Christian East*, states:

> Only *seeing* realities gives one the power to speak about
> them: "Someone who has not seen God cannot speak
> about God." In this context one can say that the origin
> of contemplation is "the spiritual sense," or "the
> heart" with its integral intuition.[34]

Integral intuition in Symeon has to do with becoming more
aware of God's presence. Indeed, it is such a deepening
awareness that one becomes united to God in and through
the realities of life and in one's own thinking, being, feeling,
moving, breathing, as divinization.

> Divinization is the fruit of repentance and reception of
> the deified Body of Christ. It involves the whole per-
> son, body and soul, and takes place in an ineffable
> manner....A person is changed entirely: immersed in
> light, this one acquires a divine mind....Then the Cre-
> ator will send the Divine Spirit; I do not say another
> soul like the one you had, but the Spirit, that is, the
> one coming from God. God will inspire you and illu-
> mine you. God will make you shine and re-create you
> altogether.[35]

In another hymn, Symeon elaborates further on the actualized state of divinization; that is, being aware of Christ as
the light shining through all reality:

> Speak, Christ, light of the world.
> Speak, O knowledge of the universe,
> Speak, Word, Wisdom, You who know
>   all in advance, see all in advance,
>   and teach us
>   the things that are useful,
> Speak and teach me the salvific ways
>   of your will
> O Savior, and of Your divine precepts!
>
> Let your light always shine upon the
>   senses of my soul to pulsate
>   mystically to Your divine words.[36]

The Soul's Senses

Symeon's words, calling on God's light to "always
shine upon the senses of my soul/to pulsate mystically to
Your divine words," are theologically vibrant. What Symeon
is describing is a living theology, an experiential mysticism
with God: "But listen to me, in order that I may show you
with actual facts what inward faith effects."[37] God is related

to the "senses" of Symeon's soul; and the senses, therefore, correspond with the soul, inwardly faithful to God's words: "Even more, the whole person, body and soul, is united to God....God unites with the intellectual soul in order to also save the mind and make the flesh immortal."[38]

Symeon is saying that such living, organic realities, functions, and approaches to reality also pertain to the spirit, the God of the universe. "For with thee is the fountain of life; in thy light do we see light" (Ps. 36:9). Symeon says,

> Light from light, light of immortality, light of the source of light, light of living water, mercy, peace, truth, the door of the heavenly kingdom; light of this heavenly kingdom; light of the wedding chamber, the nuptial bed, paradise, delights of paradise, sweet earth, crown of life, light of the saints garments; light of Christ Jesus, saviour, and king of the universe, light of the bread of immaculate flesh, resurrection, light of his face; light of his hand, his finger, his mouth, light of his eyes; light of the Lord, his voice, like light of light; light of the Comforter, the pearl, the train of mustard seed, the true one, the leaven, hope, faith: light![39]

Symeon's theology of light integrates the whole person: body, mind, spirit. Each aspect of the person is dealt with completely in terms of healing through divinization. No aspect of the person is neglected, and no dimension of the person's self is left repressed or allowed to be warped into inhumanness and lack of love toward self or others. By having every area of ourselves bathed in the light of Tabor, we are made whole and Christ-like.

Symeon focuses on Christ as the light and on the deifying light in the smallest and largest dimensions of the material and spiritual realms. Christ's finger, hand, mouth, and face are significant; this is not simply a vague spiritualized

God. Symeon wants to call forth the incarnate reality of Christ-God for each of us as mystics here and now.

Symeon gives us a timeless theology of an incarnate God to help us in the healing and deifying process. Whatever aspect of our self may need to be transformed, Symeon gives us a vision that regards no area of the human unworthy to be divinized into wholeness.

Symeon is especially useful today because so many people have turned away from established religion in search of a spirituality that integrates all levels of the sacred and the profane, as for example, deifying the profane, Buddha touched the earth in the highest state of enlightenment to symbolize bringing the sacred into its rightful place manifest in all realities.

So too, Symeon calls forth the true Christian message of Jesus walking the earth, healing and making holy all that suffered and needed divinizing. "It is God who said, 'Let light shine out of darkness,' who has shone in our hearts to give the light of the knowledge of the glory of God in the face of Christ" (2 Cor 4:6).

Symeon: A Presence of Guiding Light

Nicetas Stethatos, Symeon's contemporary and biographer, describes Symeon as a sagely spiritual guide to whom people of every description came for counsel and encouragement:

> His renown as a charismatic—as a person endowed with prophetic gifts and as one who performed miracles—led many people to him.[40]

There was nothing austere in his appearance:

> In imitation of Christ, he let everyone approach him—men, women, children, strangers or friends, no matter

who. He walked slowly and peacefully, as usual leaning on his staff.[41]

Nicetas knew Symeon personally, and the biography contains many moving descriptions of Symeon's life, including the final moments before he died, as interpreted by Nicetas. In the above description, we see that Symeon was a peaceful, Spirit-filled, approachable person.

"Peace is an inside job."[42]

We have seen that for Symeon the New Theologian, the continuity of transformation rests on a deepening awareness of God's presence within oneself and in the world around us. The deeper one's awareness goes, and just as important, the more consistent such an awareness is in one's thoughts and actions (the Chinese *hsin,* "heart-mind"), the more one is enabled to connect with the Spirit present in all life. If one does connect with the Spirit, one is aided by what the world mythologist Joseph Campbell called "the helping hands of the universe."

In Taoism, the *Tao* is untranslatable: "The Tao that can be told is not the eternal Tao."[43] The Tao is pointed to as the Way most literally, yet if one studies the *I Ching: The Book of Change,* the *Tao Te Ching (The Way and Its Power),* and the writings ascribed to Chuang Tzu, one of the masters of Taoism, one has the distinct impression that the way the Tao is spoken of is very much like the way the Spirit is described. For example,

> The...spirit never dies;
> It is the woman, primal mother.
> Her gateway is the root of heaven and earth.
> It is like a veil barely seen.
> Use it; it will never fail.[44]

The spirit, the Tao, was referred to in the *Star Wars* trilogy as the Force. George Lucas, the creator of the film series, had consulted with his friend Joseph Campbell, for a paradigm of a world spirituality in order to describe the universal spiritual journey. The Force of *Star Wars* is modeled on the Tao; and Luke Skywalker, the hero of the series, must learn to *use* the Force, to become sensitive to the Force, to learn the power of what is invisible for application in the visible world. "Her gateway is the root of heaven and earth"; therefore, to come to sense the Force is for Skywalker a journey into spiritual knowledge and maturation.

Whether in the fictional life of Luke Skywalker or in the actualized theology of Saint Symeon, to understand how the Spirit operates is to enter integral wholeness. The more one can let go of past wounds and negative patterns, the more one can enter the way of the Spirit.

Synchronicity

C. G. Jung called the phenomenon of external events coinciding with one's thoughts and interior development *synchronicity.* In Jung's Foreword to his friend Richard Wilhelm's translation of *I Ching, The Book of Change*, the word *synchronicity* is applied to what in Taoism is a very ancient concept: the more whole one becomes, the more the ego has been replaced by listening to the Spirit and flowing with the Tao, the more the events in our lives will begin to mirror our internal state.

Jung took a daring professional leap by stating his belief in synchronicity. In fact, he began to see synchronicity—learning to flow with, and discern from, events in our lives—as a mainstay of deepening personal integration. In Jung's own words:

One cannot easily disregard such great minds as Con-
fucius and Lao-tse, if one is at all able to appreciate the
quality of the thoughts they represent; much less can
one overlook the fact that the *I Ching* was their main
inspiration. I know that previously I would not have
dared to express myself so explicitly about so uncertain
a matter. I can take this risk because I am now in my
eighth decade, and the changing opinions of men
scarcely impress me anymore; the thoughts of the old
masters are of greater value to me than the philosophical prejudices of the Western mind.[45]

The prejudices Jung was speaking of came from New-
tonian physics' assertion of causality. Jung, being a spiritual
person, recognized that there was an invisible power at
work in the structures of the psyche and in the universe that
had to do with a force underlying all reality. In the words of
Symeon the New Theologian:

> God whose providence
> extends to all details,
> how is God not in everything?
> How is God not in everyone?
> Yes, God is in the middle of everything.
> Yes, God is also outside everything.[46]

Symeon also elaborates on the guidance of the Spirit:
"Learn then, friends, what is the true imprint of the seal of
Christ. You faithful ones, recognize the features of Christ's
mark! Indeed, there is but one seal, the illumination of the
Spirit."[47]

Catherine

Saint Catherine (1347–1380), who was born in Siena,
was the twenty-fourth child in her bustling family. She lived
during a tumultuous time, which included the schism

within the Roman Church, in which she became an exemplary peacemaker, and the outbreak of bubonic plague, which killed many among her family and friends.

Although Catherine was formed by the insecurities of her day, her own transformative path was two-fold. As the title of Mary O'Driscoll's biography *Catherine of Siena: Passion for Truth, Companion for Humanity,* indicates, Catherine emphasized truth and love as the mainstays of growth and recentering in wholeness and holiness. "One of Catherine's emphases in her writings" O'Driscoll notes, "is that love follows knowledge, meaning that we need to know in order to love."[48] God tells Catherine in her *Dialogues,* "From the knowledge of me to the knowledge of oneself, from love of me to love of one's neighbors." Interestingly, "while knowledge leads to love, love, in its turn, leads to greater knowledge."[49] For Catherine, therefore, the yin of love is balanced by the yang of truth. Wholeness in the complementarity of opposites is an ongoing process and learning through discernment.

Catherine's Description of the Gift of Tears

As stated earlier in this chapter, Catherine and Symeon share many descriptions of the processes involved in deepening spiritual wholeness. In both of these saints, tears are an essential element of purification and transformation, and the "sweet tears shed with great tenderness"[50] are evident as one draws into union with God.

In Catherine's case, as for Symeon, the first levels of tears are sobs for one's brokenness, the painful therapy of healing the wounds of one's past through which we all have to pass in order to be transformed. There are five levels of tears in Catherine's descriptions in *The Dialogue.* The levels beyond purification have to do with coming into the knowledge of God and learning to love without self-interest. Catherine declares that God walks with her on two feet: the first two commandments. "Remember that I have laid down two commandments of love: love of me and love of your neighbor....It is the *justice* of these two commandments that I want you now to fulfill. *On two feet you must walk my way.*"[51]

As one practices love of neighbor more and more as love of self, one enters the realm of God's heart and the internal tears of fire. Concerning the fourth and finally the fifth level, God tells Catherine in *The Dialogue of Tears:*

> Her will, drawn along on the heels of understanding, tastes my eternal Godhead and knows and sees therein the divine nature joined with your humanity. She takes her rest then in me, the peaceful sea. Her heart is united with me in affectionate love, as I told you at the fourth and unitive stage. When she feels the presence of my eternal Godhead she begins to shed sweet tears that are truly a milk that nourishes the soul in true patience. These tears are a fragrant ointment that sends forth a most delicate perfume...[and in the fifth stage] the fruit of these tears of fire is no less than that of physical tears of water....I give her spiritual tears, tears of the heart, full of the fire of my divine charity.[52]

In fact, for Catherine, tears indicate whether one's heart is alive: "Tears are the messenger that lets you know whether life or death is in the heart."[53] Without the life-giving flow of the unconscious, the flow that signals the release of the harbored contents of the past, one cannot have the tears of fire, the internal tears of life that join one to the guidance of the Holy Spirit.[54]

Loving Neighbor

Quoting Lao Tzu we read the following from the *Tao Te Ching* on a community of heart:

The Tao person dwells in peace:
Reaching out
In a community of heart,
Regarding all that lives
As one family[55]

This community of heart for Catherine has to do with staying centered in truth and love. Truth is the "cell of self-knowledge" by which one learns "to love God's goodness within yourself."[56] Therefore, in reaching toward one's neighbor, one will not be afraid to risk loving:

Come confidently; entrust yourself to Christ gentle Jesus. For if you do as you should, God will be on your side and no one will be against you. Up...courageously! I tell you, you have no need to fear.[57]

From F. C. Happold, we know that Catherine was "correspondent and advisor of popes, emperors, and kings."[58] The enormity of her message and strength came from the integration within her inner cell of continually "living in God's holy and tender love."[59] Along with the tender opening, through tears, to God's healing love came her remarkable ability to speak the truth to the leaders of her day.

Hence, we see once again the transformative bridge for Catherine between love and truth. Being a peacemaker was not possible for someone who was not grounded and "engrafted into the word who is love."[60] Love is like a tree: "All of you are trees of love: You cannot live without love because I made you for love."[61] Once we are able to love ourselves, we become capable of practicing love, peace, and truth-speaking in the world around us.

The Dalai Lama, winner of the 1989 Nobel Peace Prize, has put this spiritual reality of the inner forming the outer thus:

Although attempting to bring about world peace through the internal transformation of individuals is difficult, it is the only way....Love, compassion, altruism are the fundamental basis for peace. Once these qualities are developed within an individual, he or she will create an atmosphere of peace and harmony. This atmosphere can be expanded and extended from the individual to his family, from the family to the community and eventually to the whole world.[62]

Catherine the Peacemaker

Suzanne Noffke, one of the foremost scholars on Catherine, has aptly called Catherine a "social mystic"[63] because her prayer life and her activism in speaking the truth infused one another. Because Catherine realized through her own mystical experience the "sacramentality of all life in Christ," she treated issues of injustice as causes that denied the relationship of God's presence within all people; therefore, she tried, literally with every fiber of her being, to awaken people to the truth of particular situations in order that they might wake up God's goodness present in all life. Noffke states that one of Catherine's favorite concepts is the mystery of God's love and relationships to all people, and how that mystery reveals, through mystical experience, the Christ-filled sacramentality alive all around us.[64]

"Mystical rapture in God always gave her certitude for quick action," according to Alois Maria Haas, and she projected her internal ecstasies into "instruction and preaching about...the necessity of an uncompromising knowledge of self and of God."[65] One could not go deeper into an awareness of God without stating the truths concerning the political and personal ills present in one's world.

For Catherine, transformation always included improving the world around her as part of her own coming into wholeness. Catherine was known both for her great love and for her tremendous strength and charity:

> The tales that have come down to us from these years of "social work" in Siena are full of the warmly human side of Catherine. She served as a nurse in homes and hospitals, looked out for the destitute, buried her father. Yet this sudden shift to the outside did not end the silence and contemplation she still found in solitude. Her public activities gained her notoriety, but those who began to gather round her looked for her most of all at home in her room, where in hours of conversation she both learned and taught—learned the subtleties of theological argument and biblical interpretation, and taught what she knew from experience of the way of God.[66]

Here was a woman who had not even been taught to read as a child evolving through her own motivation and inspiration by God into one trained to understand biblical and theological expositions. Eventually Catherine's subtle knowledge would influence many leading figures of her day.

Catherine's own presence must have been a remarkable confirmation of opposites, as is reminiscent of Hinduism's teaching of *Satchitanada*.

Satchitananda

Sat is the truth, *chit* is being, and *ananda* is the bliss we experience when realizing that the closer we come to the truth, the closer we come to God. In the final unity of Catherine's life and "in the heart of *Satchitananda*, there is no divisiveness, nothing withheld or concealed from the whole."[67] The result of such an enlightenment is that "the richness of Satchitanada consists precisely in the communication of its richness; its glory is the communication of glory. This glory is given to each one and also given by each one."[68] The job of Satchitananda consists in going beyond the ego, identifying with other people and creatures as *Thou's* as well, and sharing one's awareness freely "in communication, in giving and receiving."[69]

This is why Gandhi's nonviolent warriors were called *Satyagrahi*, followers of the truth. For Gandhi, truth brought one away from violence and gave one the courage, again through identification with the *thou* of another, to fight the fight with "peace in one's soul."[70]

Gene Sharp, Senior Scholar-in-Residence at the Albert Einstein Institute, has done a tremendous amount of research on viable nonviolent alternatives. We see a new trend in diplomatic circles, the work of former President Jimmy Carter, for example, in learning how to *mediate* and to reach the ends both sides desire through nonviolent means. Sharp mentions several forms of noncooperation in undertaking nonviolent protest and persuasion "through verbal and symbolic expressions of a position or a grievance." Among these are letters, petitions, leaflets, teach-ins, lobbying, picketing, mock awards, vigils, marches, religious processions, demonstrative funerals, and silence.[71]

Sharp believes that if citizens come to the realization that "it is conceivable that whole societies can be trained to carry out this kind of resistance in defense crises, then civilian-based defense would be possible as a policy that utilizes nonviolent civilian action to protect society against internal usurpations and external invasions."[72]

During Catherine's life and at that time in history, mostly because of Catherine's personal religious convictions and experiences, she indeed practiced much of what Sharp describes. In fact, Catherine's indefatigable letter writing foreshadows the successful work of Amnesty International in freeing political prisoners and victims of injustice, largely through the practice of its dedicated letter-writing members.

In applying and relating Catherine's contemplative action, her social mysticism today, I quote Sharp: "the basic principles of the great religions, applied strategically to the world's pressing conflicts, will recall themselves also as the basis of the highest pragmatism."[73]

Evolving Socially From Within

Social mysticism may take many forms, and the best individual means of action seems to involve areas of conflict that we most passionately feel need changing. In describing Mahatma Gandhi's approach to political change, David Kinsley states that there was a parallel correlation between Gandhi's own personal purification and the purification of the world around him.[74]

Recently there were several incidents of racial hatred in the lives of my students. I decided that the best way I could help was to point out several religious insights on the theme of human diversity. I put the Buddhist proverb "We all have the same color bones," Jesus' commandment on love, Native American Irene Pyawasit's "We all bleed red," and Muhammad's "All people are equal, as equal as the teeth of a comb" on a flyer with a graphic of about one hundred ethnic groups and had these printed on orange paper. By arousing discussion among students and bringing ingrained prejudices to the fore, I hoped their minds and hearts would begin to think and feel independently of familial and societal biases. How many students, for example, realize that Jesus was a Jew and a Semite? Many think of Jesus as a blonde, blue-eyed, Anglo-Saxon, speaking in King James' English.

By pointing to cultural impositions past and present, ethnicity finds plenty of room for differences. Students awaken to an appreciation of the insights of Irene Pyawasit and the Buddha that we may have cultural particulars at work in our belief systems, but underlying those differences are ethical and spiritual intuitions that are freeing for the entire human race. It may be that one form of social action today is to affirm the multiculturalist truths that make people "as equal as the teeth of a comb."

It has become clear to me that one of my own roads of social action is to demonstrate through at least several cultures what Jesus calls "love." When students realize that technological progress may not be progress without the integration of spiritual and ethical stratagems as well, I know the fruits of reflective growth are bearing fruit. For global health and peace depend on the inclusion of spirituality, ethics, science and technology, art, and education.

Each of us has a mystical social gift gained through our prayer life. It is vital to have social commitments, whatever form those commitments may take for each of us. Someone may picket to protest an unfair law; another might be a Western-trained anesthesiologist who decides to learn about Chinese acupuncture so as not to administer as much anesthesia during surgery, someone else may become involved in hospice work to counter our culture's inability to cope with the reality of dying. Social action that lasts, according to the *Bhagavad Gita,* and does not become uninspired, is directed from within as an integral part of our total human development: "Great is the person who, free from attachments, and with a mind ruling its powers in harmony, works on the path of consecrated action."[75]

New Possibilities

Once healing begins, possibilities arise for our personal and social growth that may not have existed previously in our minds. As new possibilities emerge through prayer and

healing, social mysticism becomes not a duty but a spontaneous garden of interior flowers. The flowers' scents, colors,
and living crystalline shapes can further joy and healing in
the world. In the Taoist Chuang Tzu's words:

> Make it be Spring with everything;
> mingling with all and
> creating the moment in your own mind—
> this is what I call being whole in power,
> this is what I call being whole in power.[76]

The masters Chuang Tzu, Catherine, and Symeon call
us into an alternate definition of power, a power that is not
dominating or damaging, but rather a meditative, calm
power, bursting with multidimensional healing.

> From the mind
> of a single, long vine,
> one hundred opening lives.[77]
> > Chiyo-Ni

III

The Divine Within

I would like to begin this chapter by posing a question that I am unwilling to answer, not because I am uncooperative or argumentative by nature, but mainly because I suspect the answer (which, by the way, I don't know) is vast and complicated. The question is, why have the Western religions, including Roman Catholicism, Judaism, Islam, and most Protestant denominations, avoided the issue of deification, that is, the divine within? They have not only avoided deification, but have condemned people who professed the experience of believing they were godlike, even to the extent of murdering them.

I will name but two of these condemned saints: al-Hallaj and Meister Eckhart. The famous Muslim mystic al-Hallaj, who said "I am God," promptly had his body cut into pieces and thrown into the junction of the Tigris and Euphrates Rivers by the Orthodox Muslims of his day. He had the last word, however, for as the hagiography states, each of his chopped body parts sang from the river, "I am God," to his murderers' consternation.[1]

The other saint, Meister Eckhart, a fourteenth-century German mystical theologian, was also condemned, not only during his lifetime, but for several hundred years after. Eckhart is now having a renaissance, and has almost become a spiritual fad, if there is such a thing among the contemplative cognoscenti. Eckhart is called a Christian with Buddhist insights by Christians sensitive to interreligious dialogue. He is thought of as Buddhist in his comprehension of reality as mind and emptiness. His language for the most part is still mystically timeless, and you will rarely experience a smarter read among any other world mystics.[2]

Before we dwell on Eckhart, however, let us reiterate the question with which this chapter begins: why is there so much fear, so much denial, of the God-within-us experience in the Western religions?

This is not true of the Jewish mystical text, *The Kabbalah,* of certain interpretations of Muhammad's own sayings and the later Muslim mystics, of the Sufis, or of the Christian mystics like John of the Cross. Yet until recently these empowering spiritual experiences were rarely taught in church, mosque, or synagogue. Today one of the guideposts of fundamentalism, whether Muslim, Jewish, or Christian, is a reliance on external law and ritual and an avoidance of the interior spiritual quest.

I have no single answer to this puzzling question. Perhaps the rationale of authority, social structure, and collective obedience has played a role in the historical oppression that has had far-reaching consequences for how we live the sacred in daily life and for how entire cultures view spirituality, education, the arts, and even technology. I do know that when the Brahmans, the priestly caste of Hinduism, ceased to teach the inner truths of how to know God, and instead relied on the socially acceptable platitudes of their day, the decline of Hinduism in India spread like wildfire. Then a young prince declared that we all contain the Buddha-nature, and in his enlightenment, the Buddha demonstrated that the greater power and intuition comes through meditation not ritual.

It is a historical irony that most spiritual revolutionaries, such as Buddha, rely on the truths of the tradition of their own birth. They live the tradition in a way that either revitalizes it or creates a new religion with the same truths expressed in a more creative and individually fulfilling way.

Deification

Deification is the recognized spiritual reality that each of us contains within in order to manifest our true divine nature. Deification implies not merely a likeness to that nature, but an actual embodiment of the sacred in our own individual body, speech, behavior, and life commitments.

Deification does have its dangers. Hinduism has always recognized the danger in idolizing a guru. There have been terrible abuses in guru-disciple relationships whereby a person is extolled as a god/goddess, and forgetting his own clay feet, violates one of the most sacred taboos: that against having another person project his deepest interior needs onto one as a guru and guide, and in turn utilizing those needs for one's own ego-gratification.[3]

Several years ago I went to a wealthy and famous ashram in the United States. The chanting was wonderful; the atmosphere invigorating; the food delicious, homemade, wholesome, and succulently presented; the fees for study programs and retreats exorbitant; the public relations slick. The guru's picture on the altar was too much for me as an American bred in a democracy and having lived in countries where dictatorships spread the worst forms of herd mentality and collective vapidity. I can still acknowledge that this particular guru has unusual wisdom, an educated knowledge of the Hindu scriptures, and a dancer's grace. But she is not a goddess, and if she asked me to jump from a five-story window to demonstrate my faith in her powers, I would probably say, "No, let's see you do it!" Perhaps one of the attributes of American independence is cocky skepticism, and I believe we should be bringing that skepticism into our spiritual perceptions of the sacred as well. We would have much less of the worst New Age religion and more genuine mysticism if we brought a respectful skepticism to our altars.

The above is not a tirade, even though I can easily imagine it giving that impression. It is an elaboration of my involvement for decades in interreligious circles. As a dear friend, a psychiatrist from Columbia University, said to me, "The people in the United States, especially young people, are spiritually infantile." A guru may be a facilitator, a guide, one who shows the way to our own individuation and deification, but when that relationship is changed—and I suppose this could happen even within one's own internal process—and one abandons the intense doubt, questioning, and humility necessary for authentic self-realization and self-development, the result is a halt on the narrow path and stifling self-congratulation or flattery. On Anthony deMello's last retreat at Fordham University in 1986, he stated that one must watch for the mud of flattery and seek instead the song of the bird who leads us into the music of the universe and God's heart of compassion.[4]

The Lotus Self

On a positive note, my friend Swami Premananda, with whom I was an undergraduate, has been with her mentor Swami Satchitananda for many years since our graduation. She now has a Ph.D. in psychology and yoga, and much of her work has been on religious addiction and the path of yoga as a way to individual reliance and self-esteem. Swami Satchitananda has published numerous books, and I have met him on several occasions at the United Nations. The impressive thread in all of his spiritual work is his deep respect for the truth embodied in all religious traditions. His national and international ashrams hold the creed "Truth is One, Paths are many." The emblem of this creed holds the symbols of numerous world faiths, including one for religions that no longer exist and one for the small indigenous traditions that are endangered today.

At his main ashram in Yogaville, Virginia, the architecture expresses Swami Satchitananda's philosophy. The main building is in the form of a giant pink and white lotus, the Hindu-Buddhist symbol of the deified self arising from the swamp of ego-conditioning.[5] It is the purification process that forms the lotus self, the belief stemming from the recognition that conflict is mandatory in the flowering of insight and liberation. Each petal in the ashram contains an altar for a different world religion, where one may meditate and respectfully appreciate the truths of that particular cultural expression religiously. There are altars for Taoists, Christians, Buddhists, and Africans, the latter representing the many traditions of that unique continent.

Swami Satchitananda's teaching cultivates the inner contemplative life by trying to extricate the gems of truth from within the caves of world spirituality. One is free to choose one's own path with the help of an experienced guide. This is democratic edification, if you will—an embrace of the sacred that relies on classic spiritual necessities, such as continually becoming empty in order to touch and be the holy. In the words of Meister Eckhart:

> "Life" means a kind of seething in which a thing ferments and first pours itself into itself, all that it is into all that it is, before spilling over and pouring itself outside.[6]

In order to be one with the sacred, one must return to that interior empty state in which we understand *who* we really are, and then move into our lives with that God-life. According to Eckhart: "Before I became one thing, I was the life of

God."[7] Mystically, God is who I really am; to get back to God is to truly find myself.

Meister Eckhart

Like deification itself, "Eckhart was and is a daring and difficult thinker, a man who escapes any easy categorization, and frequently a scandal to the timid and conventional."[8] The irony of his life was the fact that he was always loyal to the teachings of the Roman Catholic Church as a Dominican teacher and preacher. Eckhart wrote in both Latin and German. The Latin works contain his more scholarly treatises and sermons, whereas the German vernacular sermons reveal a man's soul able to stir his "readers and hearers from their intellectual and moral slumber....Meister Eckhart was not only a highly trained philosopher and theologian, but also a preacher, a poet, and a punster who deliberately cultivated rhetorical effects, bold paradoxes, and unusual metaphors."[9] These characteristics of Eckhart's work also apply to his mysticism, which came from his own interior life, formed by the nuances of his intellectual training, his own originality as a teacher, and his unique ability to reach people from all backgrounds through his unique use of language.

Perhaps we may hypothesize that because of his time, his culture, and his church's fears, Eckhart's individuality of expression was not seen for what it truly was: a master's ability to express thoughts and intuitions into the stages of spiritual growth and the very composition of God beyond the limiting cultural expressions of his time. If Eckhart lived today, who would he be? How would he make a living? Would he be at the forefront of international interreligious dialogue?

Eckhartian Deification

According to Eckhart, "God is 'No-thing,' and we must become no-thing to be one with God."[10] God is the ground of all being; by limiting God through our definitions, or in Eckhart, our particularizations, we limit our experience of God *through* our categorization. God is no-thing, that is, no single being, but rather the Being that undergirds all reality.

Eckhart's "no-thing" is similar to the Buddha-nature that pervades all reality but cannot be circumscribed by one name or form. For Eckhart, as for Buddhism, the path of detachment teaches one how to let go of a thought, definition, or goal and open oneself to the God in all life who is Wisdom. As Eckhart states:

> Accordingly, it should be noted that nothing is so distinct from number and the thing numbered or what is numerable (the created thing, that is) as God is. And yet nothing is so indistinct.[11]

The twentieth-century Jewish philosopher Martin Buber spoke of the I-thou relationship as God-centered and the I-it relationship as one that is alienated from self and life. What is unfortunate in Eckhart is his emphasis on the word *thing* to define created beings. In historical hindsight it would be preferable if he had made clear the Buberian distinction between subject-subject relationality and treating subject as object with the consequential inevitability of objectifying life's experience. Despite his language, I believe Eckhart is speaking of what Buddhism does; that is, the mind subjectively influences how we experience beings as either subject or object. If we treat another being—whether a human, an activity of life, or another sentient life form—as subject, and therefore as containing aspects of the sacred, we are experiencing life as a "thou" through an I-thou relationship. If, however, we objectify our perceptions, we in turn separate ourselves from the holy in self and world.

Detachment

Eckhart appeals to Buddhists because of his emphasis on detachment as the way to subjectify experience. When we cling to a mental projection, we often cannot extricate ourselves from the projection. In other words, we become attached to the projection, and we may become incapable of perceiving reality as it is.

The entire focus on detachment in Buddhism, revealing *suchness,* creates a mental framework that does not "thingify" reality, but rather witnesses, through meditation and the watchfulness of the meditative state, the Buddha-nature, the *dharma* of the universe (the rightness of the universe's intrinsic law). The following poem, *This Mind Is Buddha,* well describes the subjective state, appreciating the suchness, the Buddha, in all natural processes:

> Under blue sky, in bright sunlight,
> One need not search around.
> Asking what Buddha is
> Is like hiding loot in one's
> pocket and declaring oneself innocent.[12]

Deification is not an acceptable term to Buddhists because the Buddha is all around; the "loot" of suchness does not have to be hidden by ritual or external laws or demeaned by attempting to objectify oneself by pretending to be innocent. One *is* innocent! One *is* born in a state of original innocence that the entire body of Buddhist koan literature aims to reteach us. *Koans* are conundrums aimed at shattering the ego's objectification. Originating in China with the Ch'an masters, who uniquely combined Taoist characteristics of parable, paradox, and humor with Buddhist teachings on mind and emptiness, the koans are a mainstay of the Rinzai Zen school practiced in Japan and the United States. Most koans are recorded in *The Blue Cliff Record,*[13] and much of the teachings on subjectivity come from these koans.

I can count on my twenty fingers and toes the major books that have changed my life. No book, however, has influenced me as radically as Erich Fromm's collection of essays in *Zen Buddhism and Psychoanalysis.*[14] D. T. Suzuki has an essay in the book that declares that "the unborn is the fountainhead of all creative possibilities."[15] This line is reminiscent not only of quantum physics, but also of Eckhart: "God is distinguished by his indistinction from any other distinct thing, and this is why in the Godhead the essence or existence *(essentia sine esse)* is unbegotten and does not beget."[16] The God beyond God is the ground of all being, all creative possibility, all life.

According to quantum physics, the subject determines what will form from the "fountainhead of all creative possibilities." A poem by the fourteenth-century Japanese poet Shutaku speaks to this very profound, complicated, and metaphysical truth:

> Mind set free in Dharma-realm,
> I sit at the moon-filled window
> Watching the mountains with my ears,
> Hearing the stream with open eyes.
> Each molecule preaches perfect law,
> Each moment chants true sutra:
> The most fleeting thought is timeless
> A single hair's enough to stir the sea.[17]

For Shutaku, when one enters the detachment of enlightenment, one attains a lucidity that metaphorically watches with the ears and hears with the eyes. What Shutaku is describing, aside from the profound, complicated metaphysical truth, is a psychological state of enlightenment whereby the unconscious becomes conscious.

Making the Unconscious Conscious

One of the most helpful concepts articulated in *Zen Buddhism and Psychoanalysis* is a definition of the enlightenment experience as psychologically making the unconscious conscious. Before I read this text, the enlightenment stories, goals, and metaphors were too esoteric for me to grasp. However, when I read Fromm's and Suzuki's essays, my Western mind "clicked"; making the unconscious conscious certainly was the road the Christian and Muslim mystics of the West had spoken of for centuries as the purification process.

Koan practice teaches one to look at one's own mind, at one's own thoughts, conditions, habits, goals, loves, fears, and inspirations. Eckhart's God beyond God, is the description of reality in one's deepest soul: "God's being is my being and God's being is my primordial being."[18]

When the unconscious is purified—that is, made conscious—we begin to live life clearly through our original, primordial being. We become childlike, innocent, free of the encumbrances of the unconscious ego-projections that often smoke our minds. When the unconscious is cleared, God's being has room to grow in our minds, souls, and lives; and we open to life as we knew it when we were very young children.

Childlikeness

Several years ago when I was giving a retreat and speaking on the spiritual theme of childlikeness, a woman came to see me. She shared that she was Ashley Montagu's niece, and asked if I was familiar with his most recent book, *Growing Young,* which he had written at Princeton in his eighties. In this delightful book the great anthropologist makes several startling declarations on human nature, on the importance of remaining childlike throughout one's life, and on his own scientific cultural observations, which some may remember from his earlier discoveries. For example, babies who are not held and loved will often die from the deprivation. In fact, for Montagu childlikeness is always connected with being loved and in turn loving others.

One may well ask, at this point, what does this have to do with deification, with Eckhart, with Buddhism? The answer is, literally everything. To quote Montagu:

> It is the childlike nature...the need to love others and to be loved, the qualities of curiosity, inquisitiveness, thirst for knowledge, the need to learn, imagination, creativity, open-mindedness, experimental-mindedness, spontaneity, enthusiasm, sense of humor, playfulness, joy, optimism, honesty, resilience and compassionate intelligence, that constitute the spirit of the child. Together these traits add up to that innocence, that freshness, that characterize the child.
>
> In other words, the spirit of the child is, in the profoundest sense, the spirit of humanity, an adaptive trait of the greatest biological value.[19]

I am reminded of a film on Buddhism in which an English searcher asks a mischievous Zen master what enlightenment is, and the Zen master quotes Jesus: "To become like a child."

For Montagu, embodying all these childlike characteristics is not just an idealistic trait of being human, it is of the "greatest biological value." Without the continual nurturing of our own and societies' childlike qualities, we suffer from "the mutilations of adultification."[20] Here the spiritual and the secular are in similar positions of objectified deprivation whereby the suchness of each instant of the sacred revealing reality is lost. For it is "those childlike qualities [that] constitute the most valuable possessions of our species, to be cherished, nurtured, and cultivated."[21]

The Role of Education

As a college professor, especially one who teaches spirituality, I am painfully aware of our students' lack of education in what Suzuki calls "the art of living."[22] Many have learned survival skills, but these skills will not protect them from the psychosomatic illnesses of stress and the vacuum of meaninglessness so many of them suffer from because of the separation of spirituality from their inner and daily lives. I have struggled for years developing teaching methodologies to help students contact their own inner teacher, their own soul-self. Fortunately, education is changing; teachers now do more collaborative learning in the classroom, learning that focuses on students not as passive learners, but as active learners in their own educational adventure.

One of my best classes each semester is the class in which students write their own haiku. This is in the course introducing Asian traditions. We study several haiku poets, partners discuss Buddhist themes in the poems, and we culminate the class period with each student individually writing his or her own verse. A sixty-five-year-old student commented on how amazed she was by the depth of nineteen-year-olds in the voices of their poems. Typical Buddhist themes of sadness, life and death, impermanence, the beauties of life, and the profane as sacred all seemed to emerge spontaneously when students felt they were not being judged. Eckhart relates this state of touching and beginning to express the divine within as the birth of the Word in the soul:

> Foster the awareness of this birth within yourself, in your ground. So that your powers will be lit up, and your outer self as well.[23]

And on the power of God in inwardly teaching us:

> As soon as God inwardly stirs a person's ground with truth, its light darts into his powers and that person knows more than anyone could teach him.[24]

"The Word of God humanified, and Thou art of the human deified"

Deification is not separate from truth, knowledge, or education in Eckhart, because God is intelligence, mind, truth.[25] Evelyn Underhill defines this rebirth and deification by quoting Nicholas of Cusa: "The Word of God humanified, and Thou art of the human deified."[26] In further elaboration on deification, Underhill speaks of Meister Eckhart as a mystic philosopher and describes the mystic birth Eckhart speaks of as the birth of the Word in the soul:

> Since the soul, according to mystic principles, can only perceive Reality in proportion as she is real, know God by becoming God-like, it is clear that this birth is the initial necessity. The true and definitely directed mystical life does and must open with that most actual, though indescribable phenomenon, the coming forth into consciousness of [the human's] deeper, spiritual self, which ascetical and mystical writers of all ages have agreed to call Regeneration or Re-birth.[27]

In his book *Visions of Innocence: Spiritual and Inspirational Experiences of Childhood,* Edward Hoffman ties the inspirational lives of people who follow their dreams to much earlier peak experiences of childhood that shaped their paths and goals as adults. The connection I am making here is between childhood characteristics and connection to God inwardly, with later mystical rebirth in life to consciously choosing to unify oneself to the sacred within and without. Once you experience this enlightenment of rebirth into deification, Eckhart states:

> All things are simply God to you, who see only God in all things. You are like someone who looks for quite a while at the sun, and afterwards sees the sun in whatever he looks at.[28]

I am reminded here of a verse by the contemporary Japanese Zen master Shinkichi Takahashi, which I read in class as we began our Zen poetry section:

> The three thousand worlds
> are in that plum blossom.
> The smell is God.[29]

Deification in Gregory Palamas

For Gregory Palamas, deification always entails the whole person. During and after his lifetime, his theological interpreters have misunderstood much of his meaning. Or perhaps, like Eckhart or Symeon the New Theologian, Palamas's message was threatening to a religiosity based on ritual law rather than internal transformation.

Writing in the fourteenth century, Palamas speaks of deification as a "luminous energy"[30] that is "ineffably present in the essence and inseparable from it, as its natural faculty."[31] When we become one with God, our senses, emotions, mental patterns are changed. We enter the mind of God as our natural faculty, and the luminous energy that is reflected in us through the Spirit "deifies the body [becoming] assessable to the bodily eyes."[32]

Eckhart speaks of this luminous transformation as a "great enlightenment," whereby "God pours into the soul such a huge amount of light, and the ground and essence of the soul are so flooded with it, that it runs over into all her powers, flowing into the outward self as well."[33]

Prayer: Living in the Mystery of God

I find it fascinating that so many Western searchers who have delved into Hinduism and Buddhism are attracted by mystical thinkers like Eckhart, Gregory Palamas, and Gregory of Nyssa. Abhishiktananda, who found union with God in India, focused on Eastern Christian mantric prayer with the breath, and on mystical thinkers of the West who vibrate in tune with the intuitions of the *Upanishads* in his gem of a book, *Prayer.*[34] Having journeyed from France to India, he was a prophetic soul who found that his own search, his own interior comprehension of deification, and his own Western prayer and Eastern meditation led to a spiritual foundation through contemplation that had global ramifications spiritually. The following is a typical jewel from *Prayer:*

> Truly speaking there is no outside and no inside, no without and no within, in the mystery of God and in the divine Presence.[35]

World religions discover the necessary ideological space here to pray and relate to one another through their contemplative experiences. No religious tradition that I am aware of ever began without a mystical revelation. Because of his own mysticism, Abhishiktananda recognized that on this level of spirituality, incorporating divine presence and deification, religionists may speak to each other. Their "thou's" call to one another clearly and compassionately, passing over dogma and cultural-societal overlays:

> Do we say: "Let us first think of the air which surrounds us and then breathe?" Willingly, unwillingly, consciously, unconsciously, we breathe and go on breathing; continuously, too, air is entering our beings. So it is also with the divine Presence which is more essential to our life, to our very being, then the air itself which we breathe.[36]

Taking Prayerful Breathers

Roshi John Loori, in a film called *Introduction to Meditation,* states that we are one of the only species that now, in our urbanized lifestyles, do not take adequate time to rest. He rightly says that even a hummingbird takes breathers. Whenever I see the film with one of my classes, I am reminded of Isaiah 30:15: "In returning and rest you shall be saved; in quietness and in trust shall be your strength." Resting gives us the mandatory mental space, allowing the deified awareness of suchness.

One of the most important inspirations posted over my desk is from a fortune cookie I received when I was eating at a Chinese restaurant with my five-year-old son. It read: "Stop searching forever, happiness is just next to you." The prayerful *suchness* of the ordinary and the extraordinary was right there, in the *suchness* of our shared meal.

One cannot escape the fact that Palamas and Eckhart were first-rate intellectuals, nor the fact that they are both giants in the field of spirituality. Yet deification is right here now, as they well tell us. It is a state of mind that is possible to experience while fumbling with chopsticks and enjoying that last sauce-soaked mushroom. Thank God, deification is not just in our heads, an idea to ponder and philosophize about. But it is rather a continuous embodiment of divine Presence within and without. In the words of Palamas:

> Can you not see, then, how essential it is that those who have determined to pay attention to themselves in inner quiet should gather together the mind and enclose it in the body, and especially in that "body," most interior to the body, which we call the heart?[37]

Mandala Practicum

I would like to turn now to the Tibetan Buddhist tradition, and to that tradition's elaboration on human deification. I point to Tibetan Buddhism as a method of demonstrating the edification of deification. From a Buddhist perspective, each of us is the Buddha. Enlightenment is, in large part, the realization that our true nature is in the Buddha-nature.

During the months of May and June 1997, many of us then living in Rochester, New York, were privileged spiritually and artistically with the creation of the *Kalachakra* sand mandala done by three Tibetan monks. The word *mandala,* meaning "magic circle," comes from the Sanskrit language. C. G. Jung believed that the mandalic circular form was a symbol of the Self's wholeness and integration. To paint and/or meditate on a mandala brings one into psychic wholeness visually represented.

Mandalic shapes are abundant in nature and art: snowflakes, sunflowers, shells and galaxies, lotuses and roses, the rose windows in Christian medieval cathedrals, the yin-yang symbol, and so forth. For instance, the yin-yang symbol is represented at the center of the Cathedral of Lyons's stained glass window.

Physiologically and psychologically, it is believed that

concentrating on a mandalic form brings the two hemi-spheres of the brain into harmony. The point is that though these opposites exist, it is only in harmony that they comple-ment one another and bring each other into completeness.

In her groundbreaking book on women and Tibetan Buddhism, *Passionate Enlightenment,* Miranda Shaw explains in detail the Tibetan use of mandala:

> One of the main Tantric images used to remodel the practitioner's subjective reality is the *mandala*. The *mandala* provides a blueprint for enlightened vision. Ordinarily each person experiences a world that reflects her cultural background, personal neuroses and attachments, and habitual patterns of thought and behavior (known as *karma*). Meditation on a *man-dala* replaces the habitually dulled way of seeing the world with a bright, crystalline world of radiant col-ors, beautiful forms, and divine images and sounds. The basic pattern of the *mandala* is a palace resting on a lotus flower that rises out of the cosmic sea. The *mandala* palace is envisioned not as solid but rather as made of crystallized light, or as translucent, like jewels with light shining through them: sapphire blue, topaz yellow, ruby red, emerald green, and diamond white. Each of the walls has a large ornamental gate and is decorated with vases, canopies, pearl garlands, and victory banners. The journey through the *mandala* symbolically re-creates the journey to enlightenment. The meditator enters by the eastern gate and encoun-ters a series of Buddhas that represent different aspects of the personality and their enlightened coun-terparts. In this process, visualization and imagina-tion are used to turn the five poisons of self-centered existence into the five nectars, or Buddha-wisdoms. Anger is transformed into mirrorlike wisdom, arro-gance becomes the wisdom of equality, desire becomes discriminating awareness, jealousy turns into

all-accomplishing wisdom, and ignorance becomes
the panoramic wisdom of all-encompassing space.[38]

The Kalachakra Mandala

The philosophy behind the Kalachakra mandala has to
do with the Tibetan Buddhist understanding of mind-heart
and the practices that arise from that understanding in
meditation and visualization.

Kalachakra was once a secret and relatively rare event
practiced only in Tibetan monasteries. Because of the Dalai
Lama's commitment to holding and restoring the indigenous religious traditions of Tibet, he has permitted the creation of Kalachakra at certain times and sites worldwide, for
the present.

I was amazed at the reverence of the general public
when people walked into the space where the three monks
were working on the sand mandala at the Memorial Art
Gallery in Rochester, New York, for five weeks. The walls
were Tibetan thematic colors: deep burgundy, burnt
orange, gold. Low chants were playing, oil lamps were lit,
and the funnels clacked together and made cricket-like
sounds as they carefully drew the sand formations. These
sensual monastic elements embraced one in a meditative
mood.

Becoming the Image

In certain lineages of Tibetan Buddhism, the
Kalachakra and visualizing meditations on certain yogi-
yoginis, Buddha-Bodhisattvas, exist to help one become the
characteristics of the enlightened beings, as Miranda Shaw
pointed out in the quotation above. It is acknowledged in
Buddhism that we all have the Buddha-nature. Meditation

with or without visualization is, in large part, a pathway bringing us into an aware state of mind that recognizes our own divinity.

The portals of the Kalachakra form the sand characters of the Tibetan *Om,* derived from the Sanskrit language. *Om* is the sound of all life, and it is our own internal identity as well. Perhaps the complete lack of fear in the Buddhist tradition toward the idea of deification may have to do with the intrinsic association between enlightenment and experiencing one's true Buddha-nature.

Buddhist Monasticism

The Buddha-nature is free, yet often thrives within and through the Tibetan monastic structures. Those structures so threatened the Maoist Chinese that when Tibet was invaded, almost all the monasteries and convents were destroyed and what is believed to be a minimum of 1.2 million Tibetans were murdered.[39]

As long as the goals of the Buddhist practitioner and the Buddhist monastic structure abide by the foundational teachings of Buddhism on enlightenment and the Buddha-nature, one is supported by the other. When an ideological system like Maoist China is threatened by nonviolence and spiritual primacy, a warping of values occurs, as the world has witnessed in China's massive destruction of the people, culture, and land of Tibet.

China, with a bizarre secular socialism, has placed its nuclear waste in Tibet. The Chinese army has raped, tortured, and murdered the Tibetans and has annihilated paintings, statues, and scriptures that were housed in over 6,000 Tibetan monasteries, some the size of small cities. These monasteries were dynamited and razed to the ground; only about a dozen are still left intact. In a final attempt to change

Tibetan identity, the Tibetan language is no longer taught, and Tibetan parents often send their children on a life-and-death trek to India, knowing that in the "orphanage" sponsored by the Dalai Lama in Dharamsala, their children will be taught Tibetan language and culture.

One More Question

Perhaps in this chapter of questions, one more may be permitted. Without the recognition of the divine within and, respect and reverence for that fluorescence, what is the priority of a people, a nation? What are the exploitive ramifications of disrespecting the values of the sacred? Is it time, perhaps, as cultural relativity has reached a peak of media mediocrity, greed, and lack of the heroic, for those of us who see the value of the Self, whether of Eckhart, Palamas, or the kaleidoscope of the sand mandala, to start asserting a human right to spirituality? It is time to assert that the divine within does exist and that when that divine is actualized, much that is beautiful, truth-filled, and loving ennobles and gives significance to the art of living.

The first chapter of Robert Thurman's book, *Essential Tibetan Buddhism,* is entitled "The Quintessence: The Mentor Worship." I would like to conclude this chapter on the validity of deification—the divine within—with excerpts from Thurman's chapter. Interestingly, it contains historic Tibetan references to males and females as mentors, demonstrating the mandalic balance of sexual autonomy and complementarity:

> You are Mentor!
> You are Archetype Deity!
>
> Source of excellence, vast ocean of justice,
> Endowed with many jewels of spiritual learning....

The outer and inner sensual goddesses
Pervade all quarters and present the glorious beauty
Of form and color, sounds, scents, tastes, and textures.

Bless me to perfect the wisdom transcendence,
Through the yoga of ultimate-reality-spacelike equipoise,
Connected with the intense bliss of the special fluency
Derived from wisdom of discrimination of reality!

This liberty and opportunity found just this once,
Understanding how hard to get and how quickly lost,
Bless me not to waste it...
But to take its essence and make it count!

For the sake of all mother beings,
I will become a Mentor Deity,
To install all beings in the supreme
Exaltation of being Mentor Deities!

Thus having prayed, may you, Supreme Mentor,
Joyously come to my crown to bless me,
Sit surely, your toenails glistening,
In the pistil of my heart-center lotus![40]

IV

In the Image and Likeness of God

Both the Western and Eastern Christian mystical traditions have focused on one profound process: transformation. The transformation of the individual into God-likeness is the means and the end of Christian salvation. To become God-like—that is, to image the divine in one's body, emotions, mind, and spirit—is to reflect the glory of the Risen Christ.

Obviously, there are basic theological differences between these two sister traditions, but they come from the same root, namely the Hebrew scriptures and the New Testament call for conversion of heart. Their shared goal is really very simple: to "go out in joy,/and be led forth in peace" (Is. 55:12).

Thich Nhat Hanh, the Vietnamese Buddhist master, makes a profoundly simple point concerning our true human nature; he says that we are meant to "be happy."[1] That happiness is our most authentic state of being. But because we allow fears, worries, and past and future concerns to dominate our thinking, we are usually not happy; instead we are uneasy, angst-ridden, and not centered.

Consider the Lilies of the Field

In the Christian mysticism of both the West and East, the embodiment of happiness is a result of the experience of God "which neither toils nor spins."[2] When we become

76

transformed by the divine consciousness within our own hearts, we inevitably experience tremendous joy. It is one of my sincerest hopes that in studying the mysticism of these two ancient Christian traditions, we will be studying the experiential reality culminating in a state of continuous joy.

This is not a "smiley face" happy; it is a deep knowing and awareness of God's presence. For Gregory of Nyssa, this continual process of ontologically growing from "glory to glory" (2 Cor 3:18) comes about through the very real experience of apprehending God.

Presence

In the parlance of contemporary psychology, presence is not merely intellectual knowledge, left-brain comprehension. Rather, experiencing the presence of God is an intuition of reality integrating right and left brain hemispheric apprehension that also embraces the intangible dimension of the eternal, so difficult for mystics to describe in language. Kallistos Ware tells us it is a "secret center of stillness."[3]

The transformation that occurs within the individual is one that is directly being influenced by the *awareness* of God's presence. The more qualitative my awareness of that presence through my breath, my body, my daily encounters with grace, the more I will image God-likeness through the calmness of my breathing and the joy of experiencing a life centered in the stillness of the sacred.

The Inner Life

Bonaventure, the thirteenth-century Franciscan theologian, speaks of the awareness of God's presence as the soul journeying back to God. Bonaventure believed that the redeemed human mirrors the divinity in terms of coming to recognize the sacred present immanently and transcendently. As he put it, "We are disposed to reenter/the mirror of our mind/in which divine realities shine forth."[4]

To image God will eventually affect every arena of our life experience. For both Gregory of Nyssa and Bonaventure, theology is impossible without the experience of God's love through presence. For these two great mystical representatives of Eastern and Western theology, the true imager of Christ is a person wholly immersed in the awareness of the Holy Spirit at work in the most simple of life's tasks. In fact, the Christian contemplative tradition generally emphasizes the point that only when one synthesizes the basic functions of breathing, eating, demeanor, and so forth with the Spirit does one come close to mirroring Christ. In the words of Bonaventure: "For every creature is by its nature/a kind of effigy and likeness of the eternal Wisdom."[5]

Mirroring Christ

When we begin our study of Gregory of Nyssa's and Bonaventure's experiential mysticisms, we will see clearly that for both the Eastern and Western contemplative traditions, imaging God is the calling of every Christian. One mirrors Christ above all through loving God in one's thoughts, for these are what influence and motivate every aspect of our being. "Finally, all of you, have unity of spirit, sympathy, love of [all], a tender heart and a humble mind" (1 Pt 3:8).

If the Christ is that deepest ground of Self that we truly are, that "place" within, immersed by calm and compassion for our own life and our neighbor's, then to be at home is to be one with the risen Christ. To feel profoundly the significance of the cross entails dying to the false ego and to such classic sins as greed and anger as well as to the unexamined prejudices of society. If we die to these sins, then we rise in the consciousness of what Christ-awareness actually means: a home for peace, a home for love, a home to embody in one's person that very unity of body and mind, contemplation and work, which *is* Christ within and manifest without through our transformed consciousness, which now truly expresses Christ's presence.

Gregory of Nyssa

Gregory came from a family of ten children, in Cappadocia in present-day Turkey. Influenced by the strong piety of members of his own family, including his sister Macrina[6] and older brother Basil, Gregory was to become one of the most influential philosophical theologians for both the Eastern and Western traditions.

Alive at a time (c. 335–395) when Christianity was beginning to be influenced by Hellenism, Gregory not only combined the Old and New Testaments with Greek thought, but also was imbued by the Jewish religious and philosophical thought of his time, especially Philo of Alexandria.

What is fascinating about Saint Gregory of Nyssa is that though versed in the most erudite philosophical thinking of his day, he never lost sight of the necessary mystical foundation for any true Christian theologian. In the Introduction to Gregory's *Life of Moses,* Abraham Malherbe and Everett Ferguson state:

> Philosophy had become religious in the Hellenistic age, and in late Roman times it had become contemplative and ascetic. The ascetic life in Christianity was a direct continuation of the contemplative life of Greek philosophy. Gregory speaks in the *Life of Moses* about a solitary's withdrawal as a "greater philosophy."[7]

The Importance of Solitude

For Gregory, solitude symbolizes and actualizes entry into God's presence. Just as Moses had to withdraw, to finally experience "an awe-inspiring theophany," so must each Christian who wishes to follow Moses' journey into God withdraw.[8]

Joseph Campbell, in *The Hero with a Thousand Faces,* speaks of three stages of spiritual growth in the journey to become transformed by the sacred: separation, initiation, and return.[9] Separation includes all I have been conditioned to follow, for example, the patterns and demands of my childhood and the norms of society. Only when I have left behind the complex labyrinth of conditioned responses, wants, and prejudices am I able to be initiated into the transcendent awareness of the God of the universe. In the following paragraph, Gregory describes the transformation taking place in Moses from separation to initiation:

> Moses lived alone in the mountains away from the turmoil of the marketplace....After he passed some time in this kind of life, the history says an awe-inspiring theophany occurred. At high noon a light brighter than the sunlight dazzled his eyes...."I will go and see this great sight." As soon as he said this, he no longer received the marvel of the light with his sight alone, but (which is most astounding of all) his hearing too was illuminated by the rays of light. The light's grace was distributed to both senses, illuminating the sight with flashing rays and lighting the way for the hearing of *undefiled teachings.*[10]

For Gregory, Moses must first withdraw into solitude in order to separate from the false layers that cover the transcendent reality of God. When Moses does encounter God, his "inner" senses are illuminated, and he becomes capable of receiving the sacred teachings therein. Moses is initiated into the truths of God-wisdom because he has separated himself from that defiled dimension of the mind and society that keeps the individual trapped in a state of semi-awareness.

Gregory continues: "The voice from the mountain forbade Moses to approach the mountain burdened with lifeless sandals." The symbolism of the sandals is that of where one's feet have been and are going. The fact that Moses' sandals were "lifeless," suggests that Moses, like all of us, exists in a state of lifelessness. Moses must remove the "lifeless sandals," in order to experience the living God: "He removed the sandals from his feet, and so stood on that ground on which the divine light was shining."[11]

We will return in the following sections to Gregory's descriptions of the initiatory stage. Suffice it to say that once the initiation occurs, a full immersion into the Source of all life follows. The final stage of return is when the individual, remade into the divine image and likeness, returns to share his or her knowledge with the community. According to Joseph Campbell, this is "the return and reintegration with society, which is indispensable to the continuous circulation of spiritual energy into the world, and which, from the standpoint of the community, is the justification of the long retreat."[12]

Epektasis

What happens to the individual who encounters the living God is a reshaping into the divinity. For Gregory, this metamorphosis is ongoing, even continuing beyond death. It is a perduring growth process. There is nothing lifeless or stagnant when one is awakened through presence:

> For this reason we also say that the great Moses, as he was becoming ever greater, at no time stopped in his ascent, nor did he set a limit for himself on his upward

> course....Therefore, the ardent lover of beauty,
> although receiving what is always visible as an image of
> what he desires, yet longs to be filled with the very
> stamp of the archetype...not in mirrors and reflec-
> tions, but face to face.[13]

Human beings cannot simply plunge into the Transcendent
without a schooling in the wise ways of the Spirit. *Epektasis,*
the Greek word meaning to "strain ahead," is a continuous
motivating and learning process whereby we are straining
to go one step further in perceiving God face to face.

We are told in the Book of Exodus that humans cannot
see God's face and live (Ex. 33:20). Therefore, from a contemporary psychological viewpoint, we would describe such
an experience of the Transcendent as having our normal
moorings pulled out from under us, and suddenly finding
ourselves without a stable anchor. In Buddhism this is
described as *sudden enlightenment.* The great twentieth-
century poet Shinkichi Takahashi, for example, had a sudden enlightenment as a young man. The intensity of the
experience plunged him into insanity. It was only after many
years that he was finally able to integrate what he had
encountered through a protracted period of solitude and
Buddhist monastic training.

It is said in Zen that a soup is tastier when simmered
slowly, as in *gradual enlightenment,* than when burned by the
hot flame of sudden enlightenment.[14]

Gregory also points to the learning and desire to
know more that is present in gradual enlightenment. However, I believe he has another meaning in mind, which is
that the Divinity is so incomprehensible and vast that even
after death we will "strain ahead" to become more and
more like the divine image and likeness. In the words of
Gregory's Twelfth Homily on the Song of Songs: "Having
thus traversed the open sea by contemplation, we might

traffic in the wealth of knowledge if...the Holy Spirit strikes our sails."[15]

Becoming One with the Transcendent

An apophatic theologian to the core,[16] Gregory is not afraid to bravely sail the seas of mystery. God's true nature is unknowable, transcendent, beyond human intelligence to comprehend. The only way to experience the living God is to open oneself to the invisible.

Mircea Eliade makes the astute observation that once the transcendent is not experienced interiorly and in the world around us, we lose meaning in our lives as human beings.[17] For Gregory, meaning and values are present only to the extent that we have purified ourselves and therein become vessels of the divine nature:

> We become like the food we have eaten. Let us take the example of a hollow vessel of crystal; anything put in it is clearly visible. Similarly, by placing the lilies' splendor in our souls, they become radiant and show forth from outside the forms within.[18]

The paradox in Gregory's thought is that the highest contemplative life is inexpressible and mysterious, yet there are certain distinct virtues that become more consolidated within our being the closer we come to God.

As an Eastern Christian, he believes these virtues are a result of the uncreated energies of God manifesting the Christ-like virtues. One cannot define God by these virtues since God's true nature is uncreated. But humans, as they come closer to mirroring the divine, will indeed embody Christ-likeness accordingly:

> A person can look at the sun in himself as in a mirror. For the rays of that true and divine virtue shine forth

in a pure life by the outflow of detachment *[apatheia]* and make the invisible visible to us, and the inaccessible comprehensible by depicting itself in the mirror of our souls.[19]

Apatheia, detachment, is the great spiritual path that leads the practitioner from the trappings of the conditioned mind into the invisible God, wherein we reflect "as in a mirror" the image and likeness of God.

The inaccessible becomes real when we encounter the mystery of God through contemplative prayer. Gregory compares this process of spiritual osmosis to John's reclining on Jesus' breast: "Having placed his heart like a sponge, as it were, beside the fountain of life, he was filled by an ineffable transmission of the mysteries hidden in the heart of the Lord."[20]

Divine Darkness

For Gregory, the awakening to the presence of the living God through light is the first step into deepening union. When Moses enters the cloud on Mount Sinai, this becomes a symbol of the desired state of union with God. The knowledge we absorb in the cloud is mysterious, unexplainable. In the words of Vladimir Lossky:

> For Gregory of Nyssa, the cloud of Sinai represents...a mode of communion with God which is more perfect and more advanced than the luminous vision....If God appears first as light and then as darkness, this means for Gregory that of the divine essence there is no vision, and that union with God is a way surpassing vision...in the awareness that the union will never have an end, that ascent in God has no limit, that beatitude is an infinite progress.[21]

The apt symbol of the cloud conveys a feeling of the surrounding presence of God, which will lead the way to Gregory's descriptions of how we receive the guidance of the Holy Spirit. What we learn in the cloud is how to see and be guided by the unseen.

It might be appropriate here, as an aside, to mention how difficult entering the divine darkness is for industrialized people. As C. G. Jung noted in the late 1930s, urbanized civilization has sought to control and develop its habitat through a one-sided rational approach to the detriment of the whole human being both individually and collectively. In the late nineteenth and twentieth centuries, technology has been one of the manifestations of such a limited worldview, which denies the feeling, sensory, and spiritual modes of perception. Technology has created its own mythos, in no way related to the true scientific tradition, and has adversely affected every conceivable aspect of existence from medicine, to education, to pollution, to food, and even to the monotonic sounds of passionless Muzak. Science itself even succumbed to a technological approach and has only recently broken away from the shackles of rigid compartmentalization with a more wholistic foundation based on the studies and observations of quantum physics. In my course entitled Global Spirituality, students are awed when they begin to learn about the organic unity of our cosmos and selves with all life, and the true scientific nature (not humanly created technocracy) of biological and cosmological reality is confronted, perhaps for the first time in their lives.[22] One student actually wept after such a class, confessing that she had always known such truths and that here, for the first time in her life, were her unspoken intuitions being acknowledged.

Gregory's divine darkness might, for example, be more easily comprehended and empathized with by many Native American spiritualities—any group, for that matter, whose lived spirituality allowed for, and gave an important role and place to mystery in the creation of their own religion and cosmology. Gregory's emphasis on darkness is well explained by Brother Casimir McCambley:

> The role of darkness, therefore, serves to create a rupture with the ordinary domain of knowledge; faith then establishes itself as the proper relationship between us and God in a realm transcending our intelligence....No mere seizure by the intelligence is depicted here, but a true indwelling or relationship with a living person in mystery.[23]

A "Perception of Presence"[24]

By analyzing Gregory's thought, one cannot avoid the fact that he is indeed speaking of Someone. Although his language extensively calls forth the imagery of Plato, especially the classical Platonic forms of Goodness, Truth, and Beauty, Gregory is a solid Christian. His mysticism of the ascent describes a *communion* with God. Gregory said of Moses, "After he entered the inner sanctuary of the divine mystical doctrine, there, while not being seen, he was in company with the Invisible."[25]

To have a true relationship with God, to find that sacred consciousness that for so many centuries gave meaning to human life, is a call to all of us. If the presence of God is hidden in the invisible, and, as Gregory states, is unknowable except through an interior commitment to discover that "dark obscurity where God is,"[26] then divine darkness is the very bridge between life and death.

For Bede Griffiths, the "degradation of the Western world has not come from Christianity...but from the rejection of the very idea of God."[27] Griffiths, who was immersed in the Eastern and Western Christian mystical tradition, was, more importantly, a mystic himself. He understood the power of consciousness in shaping a qualitative life.

Father Bede, a Benedictine, saw Gregory's theology as an ascent into divine darkness and therefore into living awareness. But he also saw clearly that because Gregory incorporated the mystery of divine consciousness as the basis of his mystical theology, he developed a cosmology synchronous with modern physics.[28]

Gregory and the Hindu *Upanishads*

> By whom shall the knower be known? The Self is described as *not this, not that.* It is incomprehensible, for it cannot be comprehended; undecaying, for it never decays; unattached, for it never attaches itself; unbound, for it is never bound. By whom, O my beloved, shall the knower be known?[29]

"*Neti, neti,* not this, not that," is the underlying apophatic foundation of one of the world's most profound scriptures, *The Upanishads.* The word *Upanishad* means "secret teaching." Therein, like Gregory's mystic, one must be initiated into transcendent consciousness.

Interestingly, the Hindu path of *bhakti,* devotional love, in combination with *jnana,* the highest wisdom, is woven through the verses of The Upanishads, just as Gregory weaves together the personal love from and for God with the deepest philosophic reflections of his time. The following verse from Gregory's *Commentary* on the Song of Songs demonstrates this combination in his theology:

> Therefore, when the soul enjoys only contemplation of Being, it will not arise for those things which effect sensual pleasure. It puts to rest all bodily movement,

> and by naked, pure insight, the soul will see God in a
> divine watchfulness.[30]

Compare Gregory's "divine watchfulness," attained once
the senses (albeit activated by the mind) come to rest, with
the following verse from the *Katha Upanishad*, in which
pleasure and pain, stirred by the desires of the mind, are
not the reality experienced. God-consciousness is:

> ...the hard-to-perceive and wrapped in mystery, set in
> the cave and hidden in the depth—[one] who, wise
> indeed, realizes this as God, by means of an awareness
> centered in the Self, leaves far behind both joy and sor-
> row.[31]

It is not that the senses are evil in any way, but the *attachment* of the mind to joy and sorrow is a hindrance to God-
consciousness. I prefer the usage of *pleasure and pain,* rather
than *joy and sorrow* in this particular translation to convey
the full meaning of an enormous energy block in the mind
through attachment to the surrendering experience of God-
consciousness. Once we begin to perceive the divine presence all around and within us, we are naked; that is, we are
free from the noisy interruptions of unexamined wants or
fears. Again, from the *Katha Upanishad:*

> Smaller than the smallest, greater than the greatest,
> this Self forever dwells within the hearts of all. When a
> [person] is free from desire, [the] mind and senses
> purified, [this one] beholds the glory of the Self and is
> without sorrow.[32]

"That Thou Art"

In the twentieth century, the Jewish philosopher Martin Buber developed the fine metaphor of an "I and Thou"

relationship to God in his book of the same title. In such a relationship, one treats, and is affected by, the "Thouness" of the sacred on every level of one's being and in every life relationship. Therefore, whether it be in my own self created in the image and likeness of God's *Thou*, or in relationship to other people, I bring reverence into all my intercommunicating exchanges.

Buber contrasts the "I-Thou" way of being with "I-It" interactions. An "I-It" mode treats self and world as an object; it is an attitude that is alienated, fragmented, certainly out of touch with one's divine nature in terms of image and likeness.

One of the truths expounded in the *Upanishads,* is *Tat Tvam Asi* (That Thou Art). The *thou* is that divine reality permeating all existence.[33] This thou of being is equivalent to truth, and thus Mahatma Gandhi was inspired to declare, "Truth is God."

Gandhi, who tried to integrate classical Hindu philosophical insights into social action for justice, realized that if one abides in God, one abides in truth. It is therefore unacceptable *ontologically* to allow a social prejudice or bad habit to cover the face of truth. This means that one rights an injustice or destructive personal habit, not by alleviating an external symptom, but through one's relationship to God as the force of truth.

For Gregory of Nyssa, as for Gandhi: "The end of a virtuous life is likeness to God."[34] In Gregory, the source of the likeness comes through contemplating God's Being as truth and love, ever growing closer to embodying God-likeness through the power of the Holy Spirit. Gregory and Gandhi reflect spiritualities that integrate metaphysical reflections into transformative everyday actions. Said Gandhi: "I do believe that the most spiritual act is the most practical in the true sense of the term."[35]

The Christian East and West

It is no coincidence that for our purpose of seeking to articulate the similarities between the Christian East and West, Gregory of Nyssa, though of the Greek tradition, is considered a major influence on the Western tradition as well, and that Bonaventure, the saint to be considered next, though of the Latin tradition, "achieved a striking integration of Eastern and Western elements."[36]

Bonaventure blends in an "organic systematic structure"—the classical Greek mystical stages of purification, illumination, and union—with the affective simplicity of Francis of Assisi's embodiment and love of the crucified Christ.[37] He created this harmonious blend theologically with an effortless structure outlined in his magnificent *The Soul's Journey into God* and *The Life of Saint Francis.*

Who Was Bonaventure?

Who was this scholarly saint who continually allowed his scholarship to enrich his inner devotional life? As Bonaventure himself states in the Prologue to *The Soul's Journey into God:*

> First, therefore, I invite the reader
> to the groans of prayer
> through Christ crucified...
> so that he not believe
> that reading is sufficient without unction,
> speculation without devotion,
> investigation without wonder,
> observation without joy,
> work without piety,
> knowledge without love,
> understanding without humility.[38]

Bonaventure has been named by the tradition *Doctor Devotus,* the Devout Teacher. Bonaventure's theology unifies all the elements of the above quotation, which are so important in creating a sane equilibrium. In this respect, Bonaventure's theology is much like the inherent balances described in the Chinese *Book of Change,* the *I Ching,*[39] whereby yin and yang must continually, through awareness, be brought into balance in one's person, diet, involvements.

In the *I Ching,* for example, reading without unction would be a failure in applying what one is learning into the praxis of living through heartfelt feeling. All sixty-four of the hexagrams that comprise the *I Ching* center on the balance of yin and yang. If one goes too far in unction, for example, one may lose one's rationality and the necessary fine-tuning of the critical intellect. If, on the other hand, one becomes extremely rational, the feeling function could be denied.

Early in his studies at the University of Paris, after Bonaventure had already joined the Franciscans, he demonstrated that he "was great in learning, but no less great in humility and holiness."[40]

In 1253 or 1254, Bonaventure became Minister General of the Franciscan Order and served in that capacity for the next seventeen years. It is symbolic, for the purpose of our study, to note that Bonaventure died on July 15, 1274, at the Second Council of Lyons. At that time he was also trying to reconcile the Greek Church and Rome. The scene of his burial ceremony was described thus: "Greeks and Latins, clergy and laity followed his bier with tears, grieving over the loss of so great a person."[41]

The Soul's Journey into God

Bonaventure's description of the soul's ascent into God is not only timeless but also pointedly appealing to modern seekers. Because of its wholistic structure, emphasizing aspects of the whole person at one with self, nature, and her own community through a transformative relationship to God, Bonaventure is a theologian who is able to satisfy the deepest yearnings of the human spirit.

Bonaventure's model for the mystical life is Francis of Assisi. Besides the official Franciscan version of *The Life of St. Francis,* Bonaventure wrote *The Soul's Journey into God,* a work based on Francis's mystical vision of the six-winged Seraph.

Bonaventure actually went to Mount La Verna in Assisi to meditate on the spot where Francis had received the stigmata through his vision of the six-winged Seraph. It was while meditating on Francis's experiences and vision that Bonaventure, with his extensive theological background, realized that the vision itself described the road to be taken through contemplation. Ewert Cousins presents the outline of Bonaventure's description of the journey:

> The vision, then, symbolizes both the goal and the journey. This symbolic interpretation of Francis's vision becomes for Bonaventure the framework of his treatise, with the six chapters tracing the stages of the journey and the seventh describing the goal of ecstatic rapture. The soul progresses along this journey by contemplating God's reflection in the material world, sensation, the natural faculties of the soul and these same faculties reformed by grace. The soul then turns to God...and contemplates [God] as Being and the Good and from there passes over into the final stage of mystical ecstasy.[42]

We have, then, an organized system describing the inner life but containing flexibility in terms of each person's individual temperament and pace. For example, Bonaventure does not say that we must pass precisely from one rung on the ascent to another; rather, depending on our background, we may skip several rungs, and then return later to wholisti-cally integrate these necessary dimensions of the human person. For Bonaventure there is no split between body and mind or between the senses and the divinity; God's pres-ence is powerfully emanating in the inner and outer worlds as a *fontalis plenitudo,* a fountain of fullness alive in every sector of life.

Bonaventure does make the point, however, in the Pro-logue of *The Soul's Journey into God,* that "the mirror pre-sented by the external world is of little or no value/unless the mirror of our soul has been cleaned and polished." Unless the eyes of our soul are cleansed, we are unable to witness truly "the rays of wisdom reflected in its mirrors." Therefore, we are strongly instructed right from the begin-ning of the Prologue to "mull [these considerations] over slowly with the greatest care." Reminiscent of Gregory's gradual awareness of God's reality and presence, Bonaven-ture states that we "should not run rapidly," for these kinds of revelations are profound and need time to germinate.[43]

Chapter One: Contemplating God
Through the Visible Universe

The contemplative path for Bonaventure often begins with an awareness of God immanently present in the book of nature. The actual title of Chapter I is "On the Stages of the Ascent into God and on Contemplating [God] Through [God's] Vestiges in the Universe." Bonaventure states explic-itly that "the universe itself is a ladder by which we can ascend into God."[44] God's being is made manifest in the "Eternal Art" surrounding us. How we come closer to God has to do with integrating a three-fold theological orienta-tion that will rectify our entire soul: "symbolic, literal and mystical, so that through the symbolic we may rightly use sensible things, through the literal we may rightly use intelligible things, and through the mystical we may be lifted above to ecstasy."[45]

Bonaventure is stating in the above quote a quite rare explanation of *how* to interpret reality in order to come closer to God. All reality has a symbolic meaning—in terms of C. G. Jung's psychology, whether lamb or wolf. The archetypes in our universe, *if interpreted with discernment,* provide a gateway to being guided by our internal self. I mention Jung here, but this symbolic approach to reality is present in most spiritualities, from Native American to Taoist. We have only to look to the art of the world to notice the profound meaning that animals, weather, landscape, and total ecosystemic patterns and relationships have provided for people connected to their place.

For Bonaventure, as for Francis of Assisi, God is present in the forms of the universe both literally and symbolically. According to both these saints, we often overlook the most common manifestations of divinity present all around us: those realities that literally, *as they are,* speak volumes about God's beingness.

In the magnificent film produced by the Smithsonian entitled *Japanese Gardens,* a poem is read that clearly explicates how within each moment a new experiential poem is created by the changing landscape of the garden itself without language, without interpretation. The water, the sunlight or moonlight, the wind or stillness, the sound of birds or frogs in the night—each frame creates its own wordless poem at that moment. Without going too far afield from Bonaventure's meaning, I do believe his use of the phrase "through the literal we may rightly use intelligible things" is instructive in terms of reverencing nature as nature is; that is, not for human gain or even elaborate esoteric meanings, but to experience, as Francis did, God present in the realities that were created to surround humans every moment of their lives.

These realities lead us into the mystical whereby we are "lifted above to ecstasy."[46] If each of us is able to quietly still the mind and be present to the reality of sky, water, birds, and flowers, we are naturally led into the mystical. Probably, before the advent of industrialization and citified concrete, humans were much more able to walk out of their doors (if they had them!) and enter the mystical through the natural world around them.[47]

In the last few centuries mysticism has become something exotic or intangible. I believe what Bonaventure was describing used to be much more accessible to people through their physical surroundings. This is not to romanticize the past and yearn for cholera or famines as well; it is simply focusing on what has recently been called "ecopsychology," and on how our place indeed influences our experience of the sacred.[48]

Concluding the chapter 1 of *The Soul's Journey into God,* Bonaventure presents a rather startling warning that if we do not pay attention to God's presence in the world around us, our abuse of "the book of creation" will lead to the natural world's turning against us.[49] Here one cannot help but reflect on the effects of pollution, pesticides, carcinogens, and so forth turning against us. Bonaventure's hope lies in our turning to God:

> Therefore, open your eyes,
> alert the ears of your Spirit, open your lips
> and *apply your heart*
> so that in all creatures you may
> see, hear, praise, love and worship, glorify and honor
> your God.[50]

Contemplating God Through the Senses

In chapter 2 of *The Soul's Journey into God*, Bonaventure describes in detail the role of the senses in helping us to perceive God through our own sacred body and the body of the world around us: "We are led to contemplate God in all creatures which enter our minds through the bodily senses."[51]

Bonaventure describes the sensory world as an "ordered Art," whereby we are given signs to come closer to the "Source" and "Fullness" of the eternal God: "From the creation of the world/The invisible attributes of God are clearly seen, being understood through the things that are made."[52] Thus, in the first chapter, God is obvious to those who are willing to experience the sacred in the world around us. In chapter 2, we have opened ourselves to the reality of the sacred in the world and now recognize that our own senses help us "enter the marvelous light of God." However, for Bonaventure, how we utilize the senses depends always on how we perceive reality. The mind is our "mirror"; if the mirror opens to the senses and does not cloud them with negative interpretations and emotions, we "reenter the mirror of our mind/in which divine realities shine forth."[53]

The mirror imagery is parallel to the Buddhist image of the mind's mirror as needing cleansing in order to experience reality with *suchness,* that is, as it is in itself. Shundo Aoyama shares her Zen viewpoint this way:

> If our ordinary, self-centered viewpoint is dominant, rocks and tree roots are undesirable. But if we change our point of view, then the very fact that there are rocks and tree roots makes the valley stream more beautiful and the sight of waves breaking upon them beyond description.[54]

The Light of Truth Glows on the Face of the Mind

In chapter 3, Bonaventure tells us that because we have experienced God through the senses and in all creatures, we now have "reentered into ourselves."[55]

With a stanza that is startling in its obvious implications as to how we perceive reality, Bonaventure states, "Enter into yourself, then, and see/that your soul loves itself most fervently."[56] For Bonaventure, the deep foundational awareness of how much God loves me, results in how much I image the likeness of the divine, because I actually come to consciously identify with God. When the "light of truth begins to glow on the face of our mind," we begin to mirror the sacred rooted in the most interior depths of our being.[57]

In the Rinzai Zen tradition, *koan* study helps one to break through the illusions of the mind's conditioning into the light of truth. There are certain *koans* that are traditionally studied in Rinzai monasteries, at levels of understanding reaching for deeper transparencies of enlightenment. The *koan* is usually put forward as a question-and-answer dialectic in one's own mind: a conundrum to confuse the rational mind in its reactive responses. Aptly described as trying to swallow a hot coal, *koan* study is an excellent resource, especially for left-brain educated Westerners, to enter that contemplative reality where "the light of truth... glows on the face of the mind."

Zen master Ummon has a *koan* that points to Bonaventure's teaching as well:

> "What will it be when trees wither and leaves fall?"
> Ummon said, "You embody the golden breeze."[58]

The appropriate response here may be to simply state that the metaphoric quality of the *koan,* especially this particular *koan,* is speaking of an experiential awareness that comes to *embody* the golden breeze. It would be un-Zen-like to attempt to describe philosophically what the golden breeze signifies. However, we may be able to go as far as saying: What does it mean that the breeze is embodied? And that the breeze is described as golden? Or better yet, let us look to a poem by Bodhidharma, to whom belong some of the most poignant *koans* and stories of the Zen tradition.

> Transmission outside doctrine,
> No dependence on words,
> Pointing directly at the mind,
> Thus seeing oneself truly, attaining Buddhahood.[59]

Chapter Four: A Remaking into Our God-likeness

On the fourth level of *The Soul's Journey into God,* our natural gifts are reformed by grace. Spiritually, this signifies that we have opened ourselves to God's transformative power, freely given through grace, to have our individual gifts reformed into their true God-likeness. No longer held back by the layers of conditioned ego patterns, we open ourselves through trust and love to transformation. In Bonaventure's words:

> It seems amazing
> when it has been shown
> that God is so close to our souls
> that so few should be aware
> of the First Principle [God] within themselves.
> Yet the reason is close at hand:
> for the human mind, distracted by cares,
> does not enter into itself....[60]

According to Bonaventure, a balanced order exists not only in the outer universe but in our internal development as well. We grow spiritually when we follow the "three-fold law" described scripturally: the law of nature, scripture, and of grace. Bonaventure elaborates on this threefold law as first, the purification of our nature necessary for an upright life, living the basic ethical tenets of the tradition that clears the way for internal transformation. Second, we are transformed, and thereby illumined, by a clear understanding of the scriptural teachings. And third, clarity of understanding is the door through which we enter the perfection experienced intuitively as "spiritual ecstasies and sweet perceptions of wisdom."[61] Nature, scripture, and grace are, then, realities we continuously interconnect in our spiritual remaking through the ebb and flow of our own needs and temperament. "Holiness of mind and body" becomes more and more embodied in our person, and our mind becomes like the "house of God...inhabited by divine wisdom."[62]

In conclusion, the remaking of who we have come to be is a remaking into our true God-likeness. Since this is so difficult to achieve by ourselves, Bonaventure describes a classical understanding of God's grace as a way to help us surrender our controls and ego-walls and allow God to work with us. Grace calls on us to "let go and let God," and the "inner sweetness and spiritual joy" that results in our surrendering helps us to continue to allow the Spirit to illuminate our mind and carries us in "the depth of discerning wisdom," through the ebb and flow of activities involved in living a joyful life.[63]

I Am Who I Am

In chapters 5 and 6 we encounter God's Beingness. We come face to face ontologically with "Being Itself" as the "first and last," the "eternal and most present."[64] We have come to experience the image and likeness of God in all creation, including our own body and mind, as well as diaphanous being translucent in flowers, birds, and the cosmos. We have been transformed through God's grace, recognizing our individual identity in a new role grounded in mirroring reverential values and goals. Now, on the fifth and sixth stages of the ascent, we are ready to recognize God's Being "whose center is everywhere/and whose circumference is nowhere."[65]

God as Being and Goodness enters reality as "self-diffusive," that is, "totally present everywhere and nowhere contained."[66] Once we enter into the presence of the sacred in the magnificent image of Bonaventure as "the book written within and without," we enter into a continuous state of mystical ecstasy.[67] The ecstasy experienced is partially caused by a constant underlying awareness that *God is presence.* When we consciously experience God within and without as One, we cannot help but be ecstatic because, as Bonaventure quotes Augustine, we will honor "the course of being, the basis of understanding, and the order of living."[68]

As we saw in Gregory of Nyssa's image of Moses as the paradigm of the human experiencing God, so too Bonaventure quotes Moses and uses verses from the Book of Exodus. We might note here, as we did in the section on Gregory, that Hinduism's *That Thou Art,* contains a mystical corollary in Exodus: *"I Am Who I Am"* (Ex 3:14). Just as the verses from Exodus speak of God as "I Am," the One, so too *The Upanishads* speak of God as One without a second. From the *Kaivalya Upanishad* we read:

> In me alone originates the All,
> in me the All is established,
> in me all things come to rest.
> I am that Brahman [God] without a second.[69]

Compare this Upanishadic verse to Bonaventure's "Therefore that being which is pure being and simple being and absolute being is primary being, eternal, utterly simple, most actual, most perfect and supremely one."[70]

It Is Enough for Us

In chapter 7 Bonaventure, describing the final rung of the ascent, declares that now we may rest in union with God. We have come to realize that oneness with God is enough for us; all reality, when founded on such a spiritual reality, becomes infused with the "illumination of heavenly wisdom"; that is, our "mind has been trained so that it may reach the Sabbath of rest."[71]

Steeped in his usual biblical references and symbolism, Bonaventure speaks of the Sabbath as an interior contemplative state synonymous with union. Employing terms like *wayfarers* and *arrival,* he points to contemplation as truly a journey into God. When we do "arrive" in God, we find that we in ourselves have become the person of peace. This peace of Christ sent into the world is experienced through a "mystical wisdom...revealed by the Holy Spirit."[72]

Although the joy described by Bonaventure is called "ecstatic," it is a joy grounded in silence and peacefulness. And like Gregory of Nyssa, Bonaventure, in the deepest of mystical states, calls upon the imagery of divine darkness and unknowing:

> For transcending yourself and all things,
> by the immeasurable and absolute ecstasy of a pure mind,
> leaving behind all things
> and freed from all things,
> you will ascend
> to the superessential ray
> of the divine darkness.[73]

Bonaventure actually says in the last verses of *The Soul's Journey into God:* "Let us, then, die and enter into the darkness." He goes on to state that death is one of imposing "silence upon our cares, our desires and our imaginings." When we do go through such a continuing crucifixion, we realize that God "is enough for us," and in a very contemporary conclusion of a thirteenth-century mystical masterpiece, Bonaventure states we will then, "Let it be, let it be."[74]

Bird Banding Practicum

The Braddock's Bay Bird Observatory on Lake Ontario conducts bird-banding projects throughout the year, depending on different bird species migrations. My son Harrison and I had the privilege of participating in banding songbirds for two mornings.

There are many ecological and scientific benefits to banding birds, such as being able to determine healthy bird populations and successful migrations. The aesthetic and spiritual advantage for Harrison and me was being able to be with so many unusual songbirds. There were mourning warblers, indigo buntings, red-eyed vireos, American goldfinches, among others. We were also gifted by being actually able to hold each songbird in our hands, feel their heartbeats, and gaze into their energetic eyes.

The spiritual practice I tried to bring to those two bird banding sunrises was first, not to bring anything with me to read, and second, to stay open to the continual flow of different birding events. If I had cluttered the experience with outside impressions, the immersion of birding with its special mood and activities would not have been as memorable an experience.

Contemplative Emptiness and Nature Practicums

It was actually through Harrison's kindergarten teacher, Barbara Crawford, that we were given the opportunity to go birding. She encouraged Harrison to go, even though he would be absent from regular schooling. She knew in advance that Harrison would learn a tremendous amount from the hands-on learning of bird banding in a natural setting.

The quiet atmosphere, the doctoral students in ornithology and the dedicated retirees voluntarily gave Harrison and me one-to-one instruction on placing the band on a bird's leg, weighing a bird, checking for body fat, and, finally, releasing a bird back into the wild.

Hands-On Learning

The integrated knowledge of spiritual openness through birding is related to Bonaventure's book. Revealing God's language as embodied in birds and their natural, wild setting created a camaraderie among people working together to help another species, and ultimately gave the gift of songbirds to future human generations by trying to preserve different species, their migratory routes, and their nesting environments. Combined with the absence of agitated busyness, humane work, steady and committed activity, the good spirits and humor, and the delicate beauty of over three hundred songbirds; this experience struck me as finely spiritually integrated. That is, it was grounded in an appreciation of the sacredness of "birdness" in conjunction with a human commitment to preserve that divine beauty.[75]

One of the doctoral students who was showing Harrison how to weigh a catbird had the catbird poop on his hand. I had to share with the two of them Issa's famous *Haiku* on the union of the sacred and the profane:

> If you are kind to them
> The little sparrows will
> Poop on you.

Right Livelihood and the Practice of Work

One of the eightfold paths in Buddhism is Right Livelihood. There is a practice in Buddhist and Christian monasticism of bringing together contemplative prayer/meditation in balanced time slots during the day's schedule with activities that either help the monastery exist materially or take care of the details of individual and community living. For example, some Trappist monasteries sell baked goods. Another example might be remembering one's breathing and mental mantra while cleaning the toilets or gardening. The purpose of right livelihood, as I understand it, is to attempt to bring one's spirituality into the practice of one's work.

When Harrison and I were bird banding, I felt that the people there, who included a spectrum of ages and backgrounds, were truly practicing right livelihood—whether as a career, in the case of the doctoral students or, for the retirees, just for the love of birds. The alive bird-shapes, the harmonious atmosphere, the spring colors, the flow of time and space, and most of all, the importance of leisure in the work itself—all contributed to the spirituality of the experience.

One could not rush a bird. For instance, one had to be gentle in removing the birds from the nets into which they fly, so as not to damage these amazing creatures, so fragile yet so strong—some migrating from distances as far as South America to Canada.

A Four-Day Work Week

It was somewhat of a revelation to witness the absolute necessity of slowness and leisure in bird banding. I thought back to the Tibetan monks creating the *Kalachakra* sand mandala, remembering how they could not rush or the sand would move into directions that were not an aspect of the wholistic design. The monks also had to regulate their breath, for the air itself could move the sand granules.

Whether in birding, creating a sand mandala, or attending kindergarten or another grade in school, the importance of leisure in truly grasping a life lesson became more and more obvious. It seems to me that even the ABCs cannot be rushed. I was leisurely pondering these thoughts when a grade-school teacher commented to me after Memorial Day weekend, "I wish we always had four-day work weeks." She smiled, and I turned to her and said, "I take that very seriously. I really am beginning to believe that all of us in this culture, children and adults alike, would benefit qualitatively if we had more time to digest our work, lessons, interactions."

It is not a positive observation that work and school weeks keep making more demands on our time. And I believe it is true that people produce more exponentially if given more quality time to put together the pieces of their lives.

When I recently gave a guest presentation to a graduate education class on "The Implications of World Religions in American Education Today," I emphasized comprehending Asian religions by experiencing some of the meditation techniques. The entire question of meditation naturally brought the group to the implications of cultural impositions in their own work of teaching. Several teachers in the group were distressed because they did not know how to bring time and leisure—that is, meditation—into their schedules.

I made the comment that I have the same problem, but since I have been focusing on the importance of leisure, I try to make my commitments like a mandala of prioritized concentric circles. In the center is remembering to take care of my relationship with God, with my true Self. Quiet time and reflection demand, in my life situation, that I choose to arise at 5:00 A.M. Only then do I have time to hear the silence, be with my God-center, and be fortified to face the adventures of the day. I also try to walk every day for at least forty minutes with our dog, and many times my son likes to join me. I conclude the walk with yoga stretches because I often have a backache from my sedentary lifestyle.

The next circle, really on a par with the first cornerstone circle, corresponds to relationships in my family, which I try, as much as is possible, to keep joyous and free from oppressive obligations. I hope that my professional projects in research, teaching, and writing enrich my family life. Next is the circle of friends and inspirational activities, and so on.

Because of my writing, I may not exercise as much as I believe would be beneficial or go to as many extracurricular events as I would like, but I spend the time I believe is essential with my family, friends, and my work. Perhaps I will exercise more and attend many more concerts when I retire.

Back to Gregory of Nyssa

I try to remember that the center of the mandala is what Saint Gregory defines as "Christ who is the power and the wisdom of God....The mystery of the tabernacle which encompasses the universe....Everything visible and everything invisible."[76] By taking the time to contemplate "the ineffable secrets" of my Christ-center, I keep my priorities straight, clear, and pure.

Gregory makes a fascinating comment, so appropriate from one of the foundational influences of Western monasticism, on the union of prayer and work:

> So the heart becomes the symbol of contemplation, and the arms of works...to provide a teaching for the higher life, namely that practical philosophy should be joined to contemplative philosophy.[77]

The arms symbolize, literally, our projects in life. When I teach, I gesture with my arms; my son is learning to write with his hands; how gently we held the birds made for successful banding. Combining the arms with the heart, Gregory's symbol of contemplation (a large percentage of his leisure time) results in living the teaching of "loving what we do."

Loving what we do stays alive through unceasing prayer,[78] through the mutuality of prayer-work. When we pray and work, we move through our lives without rushing past people's eye-souls, the prismatic dew in the morning grass, the fun and joy of being "kind to the little sparrows," so that when they poop on us, it somehow seems "right" in that particular time and that particular anointed setting.

V

Spirituality and the Arts

In this chapter, I would like to elaborate on that ageless marriage in so many cultures between spirituality and the arts. In the Christian West, the tapestry of sacred music is a path leading to a deepening, ongoing relationship with the presence of God. In the Byzantine East, the golden, ponderous tradition of iconography, like the famous Vladimir Madonna, gazes contemplatively with a bittersweet expression, fearlessly facing life's tragic crucifixions and, paradoxically, the Christ child in her arms, a mother's greatest joy. The Christian East also has the music of the soul, which even contemporary composers like Sergei Rachmaninoff (1873–1943) in his Russian *Vespers* conveys so well. And how could I even begin to elaborate in one chapter on the Western tradition's examples of sacred painting: Leonardo, Michelangelo, Matisse, and Chagall's chapel, which I viewed in Southern France on an early summer day and where I tangibly experienced his pleasure in life and his comprehension of life's darker personal burdens. There is vast richness to be explored in these two Christian traditions combining the arts and spirituality.

The main artistic experiences that have shaped my spiritual thrust were my childhood experiences. When I look at my attraction to Western mysticism, I remember the endless six A.M. masses in France—the scattered quiet of the few worshipers, the red and blue aliveness of the flickering candles, the hushed responsorial whispers at that early hour. I remember the hand of the Risen Jesus—open, outstretched in the classic symbol of "Fear not, it is I"—and the glory of France's devotion to the Sacred Heart—still pierced after resurrectional glory, but statuesquely noble like the life of Jeanne d'Arc. Whether it be true of France as a whole, or only my own subjective childhood observations, the maternal protection of Mary in painting and statue and the compassion of the Sacred Heart led me, from my earliest years, into a surrendering trust. God had the eyes of a loving mother and the call into life of Jesus who had suffered in the extreme and still, through gesture and word, said "Fear not. I am with you."

My mother's recollection was that she went alone because it was so early in the day (and safe, I might add). And when the mass was underway, she would hear the click-click of my sandals as I entered that sacred space and time. Now when I ritually experience prayer and meditation in the early hours, the softness and safety of those memories must still be pulsating in my quiet heart-soul.

My mother would then take me with her to the café, where she would have her espresso and I would relish a hot chocolate and croissant. Praying always made me hungry! The combination of the city awakening while we enjoyed our breakfast, with the early experience of sacred trust, gave me a continuous mindfulness of the unity of the sacred in the most ordinary experiences of life, whether breakfasting, showering, putting on shoes, or standing in the damp coolness of the numinous chapel.

These experiences were not coming through to a child who had not experienced pain. In fact, I wonder if their meaning-filled poignancy was not dipped in the suffering I had witnessed early on. We lived in France in a kind of traveling see-saw with the Middle East. My father was Ambassador from France to Lebanon; therefore, we were in Lebanon for three different wars.

I mentioned in my earlier book, *Christian and Islamic Spirituality: Sharing a Journey,*[1] that my hope in writing that book was that these two great monotheistic traditions, through their mystical and contemplative saints, might clearly see the similarities at the core of their shared spiritualities. That weary hope came from having witnessed so much needless suffering during my childhood.

I would like to share just one incident to convey the agony of those times. My philanthropist Uncle Gene had founded a radiology clinic in the Muslim section of Beirut. Most, if not all, of his patients were poor Palestinian refugees. My brother and I would often go to help him. Uncle Gene was not a particularly patient man, but he was very interesting to us at ages six through thirteen when we were in Lebanon. At various times he had, for example, saved from the streets of Paris a starving violinist, Albert Rozsa, who had run away from the Budapest Symphony. Rozsa and my mother, Alice Jaoudi, who was a concert pianist, would put on concerts in Beirut. Uncle Gene and my mother would have us listen to music nightly on his record player in his library. He would also take us on archaeological digs; the entire downstairs of his home was an Egyptian and Middle Eastern museum. In other words, he was a Renaissance person. Since he had no children, we felt and were treated like his own children.

The wars blazed, bullets zipped through our apartment, my mother was kidnapped and jailed, and my brother and I were pursued and taunted by a bizarre war-warped man at our apartment door that very day while no adults were around. And then one night terrorists blew up Uncle Gene's clinic. No one knew if they were Christians or Muslims. Uncle Gene's apartment in Beirut was atop the clinic, so now he and my aunt stayed with us. Uncle Gene was never the same after that bomb destroyed his greatest effort; he shuffled around the apartment at night, and he eventually lost his health and died of leukemia, perhaps from being exposed to so much radiation during his medical career.

The abyss of his loss for me is like the wound portrayed in the Sacred Heart. The vision of Uncle Gene's compassion endures, more so because he was broken and abandoned by terrorists. Uncle Gene had brought us tremendous educational pleasure in witnessing Rozsa lifted into new musical life, in the Phoenician heritage we discovered in the coins of Byblos, in the swims in the Mediterranean Sea.

The Maronite Rite

While in Lebanon I was also blessed with many positive experiences, especially the daily early morning rite that changed my mental perceptions and centered me each day in the divine presence. One of Lebanon's oldest Aramaic denominations is the Maronites. My great-grandfather could trace the lineage of Maronite priests in our family and village for sixteen-hundred years. I only mention this because a friend, familiar with world cultures, said he thought that was one of the oldest traceable lineages in the world.

When we would go to the mountains, we would rise early to attend the village church services. The air would still be succulent and the sky that almost oceanic blue right before the shock of dawn coloration. The aroma of thyme, basil, mint, and lavender was heavy, and no one felt the need to speak during our hushed procession.

I believe I did indeed experience a profound mysticism during these occasions. The walls of the church were velvety with the black soot of centuries of candles burning. The incense verged on making me ill, since I had an empty stomach, and the icons winked at me in the changing shadowy light of this catacomb-like interior. According to David Goa, speaking on the *Mantra: Hearing the Divine in India,* the sacred creates an "intimate integration." When the priest would whisper the Aramaic words, only some of which I comprehended, the "sounds put me right in the center of awe." I cannot help but make a connection between the horrid war experiences and the liberation of spirit I experienced in that ancient village setting. When we would walk home, the mountains were purple with light, women were squatting by low brush fires twirling large pita breads as they cooked, and the merging of the mundane and the extraordinary took place in my child's heart-mind, a "liberation from some dreadful bondage."[2]

In encapsulating these memories, I am left with the image and sound of Easter dawn. After all, it was not far from these mountains and this same sea where Jesus was resurrected and where he fed his disciples their Easter breakfast in his risen body. On Easter morning the villagers cup their mouths and sing from mountain to mountain, *jebel a jebel*, "Christ is Risen." Come to the feast of ordinary fresh-grilled fish and bread, and a dawn always new.

Byzantine Humanism

In *The Icon: Its Meaning and History,* Mahmoud Zibawi speaks of the Vladimir Madonna as having "an ethereal chiaroscuro [that] bestows a human warmth upon her face."[3] I find it most interesting that Zibawi's references for the twelfth century, for example, are contemporary ones. He quotes artists like Henri Matisse, who visited Russia in 1911, stating that "your young students have here, at home, incomparably better models of art...than they will find elsewhere."[4] Zibawi also quotes Giacometti,[5] and the poet Yves Bonnefoy speaking of:

> ...the spiritual Byzantium
> the place where the heart can regain possession of itself,
> sing when it might be tempted to complain,
> and rediscover a choice.[6]

The Vladimir Madonna is often cited as the icon of contemplatives. She is teaching us about the human condition, that bittersweet paradox of existence, from within. "There is no sentimentalism in the calmness of the look";[7] her attentiveness to the moment, the incredible tenderness of the icon, demonstrates her total being in the eternal now. "Woven of the transcendent features of the new creature who has been totally deified, her face, full of celestial majesty, carries, nevertheless, the whole of humanity present as well."[8]

The Vladimir Madonna is frequently called "The Mother of Tenderness," and I find it a fascinating connection, having just arrived back home from a conference for college professors in Minnesota entitled "Teaching from Within," since the keynote speaker, the Quaker Parker Palmer, stated that "academics should desist from associating intelligence with razor-like laser eyes, but rather, gaze at their students with the 'soft eyes' of contemplation."

Many years ago, my friend, the Benedictine contemplative Brother David Steindl-Rast, taught me to "gaze right into the eyes of my students." I never forgot his lesson, especially since he himself has touched so many people over the years on retreats, in workshops, and at seminars with his "soft eyes" that always seemed to me to contain the compassion of Jesus and a Zen twinkle.

Teaching From Within

On a cool Minnesota summer morning, Parker Palmer addressed our group of open-hearted, open-minded learners and teachers. Since this chapter intertwines vastly differing world religious and artistic cultures, I would like to mention how American Minnesota seemed to me: the open spaces; the unusually friendly people in town, the fried potato dishes, mushrooms sautéed and served with just-baked bread and real butter. Our hosts even had a dance on Saturday night with a group called "Global Pop," with danceable music from around the world, especially from Jamaica. I have yet to be in a country that, at least in certain circles, is as receptive to other world cultures as is America. That spirit of learning receptivity was a mainstay of our conference, which seemed to embody the heart of true contemplation.

Parker made a sagacious point that ties into American democratic idealism. He said that "intimacy as love does not annihilate differences."[9] In other words, we as individuals "allow the other to be what the other is." He included all sentient life in this definition, and I remembered how years ago, while I was at the Quaker Retreat Center in Pendle Hill, during an hour service that was accessible to spontaneous sharing from any of us present, the only being that spoke during that shared communal hour of contemplative prayer was a cricket.

The icon silences our ego-noise and helps us enter the world of self-revelation—a world where crickets speak a language we understand, where the *Theotokos,* the bearer of God, becomes us as Mother-divine: contemplative, serene, looking at reality without sentimentality, and somehow, incomprehensibly, able to live with that Truth.

Teaching from within is iconic; it is a state of being unafraid of silencing the distractions of mediocrity. It is an inducer of ultimate knowing, strong in vulnerability, soft eyes grounded in the solidity of cosmically seeing into the archetypal realities of one's own existence and the jewels of cultural expression. These are the Irishman W. B. Yeats's "monuments of unaging intellect," for him reflected in "the holy city of Byzantium":

> O sages standing in God's holy fire
> As in the gold mosaic of a wall,
> Come from the holy fire, perne in a gyre,
> And be the singing-masters of my soul.[10]

Mystagogy

Mystagogy is defined as the initiation into divine mysteries. The process of creating an icon has a mirroring quality that is mystagogical. The iconic artist first prays and fasts, usually for several days, before initiating the painting process. Chinese and Japanese paintings and calligraphy are created with much the same contemplative preparation. The artist meditates and fasts, allowing the emptiness within to grow so that the fullness of the emerging archetype may be present in and of itself without any of the ego's pretensions or interferences. For the artist, the form will emerge within the structure of time and space as a natural pattern. A mountain, old trees, crows, a persimmon, a thought in a word or sentence are painted with the ability, through brush, to capture the Emerging Mystery.[11]

For the iconic artist, the religious archetypes exist in the rich pool of biblical scenes, the lives of saints, theological mysteries, the internal mirroring of the Mother's face or the Christ's resurrection. She or he waits, listens, gazes within. When the time arrives, she may apply gold leaf to a prepared panel and then grind her own pigments from rock-like minerals. The mystagogical bridge between the ordinary pigments and the extraordinary image alive in the artist's mind is perpetuated by the painting process. The union of heaven and earth is in the creator's hands, in the mind's eye, in the slow and steady attentiveness to the details about to bring forth a universal form.

The gold leaf is usually placed first, at least for many contemporary icon painters, disclosing the secret of spiritual artistry: that the value of spiritual centeredness must come first. The praying, the meditating, the fasting, the individual communication with God one-to-one come first. The details are painted last, like the details in our lives that may only be created lucidly when we are centered.

Transfiguration

Iconic painting is an art form founded on transfiguration. It is no coincidence that one of the most favored biblical conceptions, on which so many Eastern Christian theologians have based their entire theologies, is the resurrection of Jesus. There are diverse depictions: the actual resurrection; the transfiguration, when Jesus still in human form became all light, showing his divine resurrectional form; or Jesus raising Lazarus from the dead. The resurrectional theme is the iconic philosophy: the human is sacred in a divinized body. The icon images our true earthly/heavenly, body/spirit nature. We are one when we become embodiers of the sacred presence. We become graver, happier, nobler, sillier.

Perhaps the great Muslim Sufi Rumi conveys the elusiveness of this resurrectionally alive state best through poetry:

A Chickpea Leaps

A chickpea leaps almost over the rim of the pot
Where it's being boiled.
"Why are you doing this to me?"
"You think I'm torturing you,
I'm giving you flavor,
so you can mix with spices and rice
and be the lovely vitality of a human being.
Remember when you drank rain in the garden.
That was for this."
Grace first. Sexual pleasure,
Then a boiling new life begins;
and the Friend has something good to eat.[12]

How Rumi is able to express the seriousness of the spiritual journey, the slow processes, "Remember when you drank rain in the garden, that was for this," grace, the mystical marriage, the birth of new life. And we see, not a denatured chickpea, but a transfigured feast that has become "the lovely vitality of a human being." The sensual and the spiritual are one, softened through the cooking process that breaks open the hardened legume and creates "something good to eat."

In numerous Resurrection icons, the Christ leans toward the suffering, bending out of his luminous circle to bring them in. He grasps them by the wrist, releasing them from the chains of suffering, and drawing them into the circle of the luminous self. The circle, as C. G. Jung noted, is a symbol of the Self. Here we see depicted the new life and radiance we experience, once we have stepped into the circle of archetypal forms, the circle of light.

Because of the age of several of the icons, the colors have a royal, subdued effect, which is as powerful as bright, fresh colors, but suffused by the ripening power of time and wear. In Japan there is an entire authentic tradition founded on the appreciation of aging, as in the Zen gardens whose moss and trees spend time softening, enclosing, expanding, like life itself, or in the magic of an old vessel, greenish and burnt with time, as if layers of meaning are contained therein. Wrinkles and growths, whether on people or trees, demonstrate their endurance and solidity despite existential vagaries.

The grays, burgundies, and singed oranges of the *Anastasis,* resurrectional icons, are a call to gaze. One cannot just indulge in a quick passing look. One is drawn in, heart and soul, eye and mind; and the luminous circle still shines the brightest at the center.

Christ's expression is very important as well. He is not detached; he looks genuinely, if not earnestly, concerned. This is not a God reigning on a throne looking down on "his" people, but a God who has been there, and who wants to help from his own heart and human experiences. The gaze is a bridge, just as Christ's hand is a steadying force for the incoming person. Watch how the following poem says it all:

Mirabai and Resurrection as Internal Union

> *All I Was Doing Was Breathing*
> Something has reached out and taken in
>   the beams of my eyes.
> There is a longing, it is for his body,
>   for every hair of that dark body.
> All I was doing was being, and the
>   Dancing Energy came by my house.
> His face looks curiously like the moon, I
>   saw it from the side, smiling.
> My family says: "Don't ever see him again!"
>   And implies things in a low voice.
> But my eyes have their own life; they laugh
>   at rules, and know whose they are.
> I believe I can bear on my shoulders
>   Whatever you want to say of me.
> Mira says: Without the energy that lifts
>   mountains, how am I to live?[13]

Mirabai was a devotional poet of thirteenth-century India. When I was working on my master's degree in Asian Studies, I wrote a paper on Mira for the Indian Literature course. Mira hears the call of resurrection, the transmutative Divine Lover, and drops the mediocre to follow the light of life. All of her poems are autobiographical, and the integrity of her spirit comes through in the last line of the poem: "Without the energy that lifts mountains, how am I to live?"

Mira has no choice; she is an embodiment of the mystical lover archetype of such historical figures as France's Jeanne d'Arc and Iraq's Rabi'a al-Adawiyya. Robert Bly makes the comment that this integral spiritual mysticism of lovers even made it to Emily Dickinson's house, blowing in the window through the wind at Amherst:[14]

Wild Nights–Wild Nights!
Wild Nights—Wild Nights!
Were I with Thee
Wild Nights should be
Our luxury!

Futile—The Winds—
To a Heart in port—
Done with a Compass—
Done with the Chart!

Rowing in Eden—
Ah, the sea!
Might I but moor—Tonight—
In Thee![15]

Perhaps I should learn to make the leap between Emily Dickinson, the delicate New England solitary and the wild, free-floating Mirabai, her ankle bells singing, her family's horror following her with murder attempts and evil intentions, the mild American whose fire burned interiorly resonating with the wild *bhakti* poet openly defying social convention. All of this reality is resurrectional, if not directly, certainly containing the call to change, to be, to develop, to be free. No one has moved me with her genuine freedom as much as Mirabai. She carried the circle of self on all her travels, during her meetings, and in her work, those glorious poems.

Music: The Secular as Sacred

I cannot separate the mysticism of French mornings and Eastern Rite mountain blessings from my earliest musical influences. When I was three years old, my mother took me to the New York City Ballet Company because she had taken me to a dance recital of the Jose Greco Company and later, when we went to the Greco's apartment—they were friends of our family—I had danced several of the pieces from memory. It was determined then and there that I was a child prodigy. So began a childhood career of mostly classical ballet, with turns here and there into modern dance. Eventually, in college, I became a philosophy major and left dance professionally, but I still did liturgical dance to the music of Bach. It is difficult to convey in a few pages a childhood of traveling, war-torn, and absolutely brimming with mysticism and music.

I became an early ecstatic. Sometimes in church I would enter a state of timeless consciousness, once seeing the gold circle of the tabernacle expanding to encompass the cosmos. Later, as a graduate student, I read in Teilhard de Chardin of a similar mystical vision he had that helped him create his cosmology of Christ-consciousness in union with the laws of science. Along with churchgoing, I had almost daily the blessing of great surges of union through music and dance. It was often said that my dancing had much feeling, and I suppose I could not have survived the negative feelings derived from war if I had not been graced with music *felt through my body*. Thus plays "The Music" by Mirabai:

> *The Music*
> My friend, the stain of the Great Dancer
>   has penetrated my body.
> I drank the cup of music, and I am
>   hopelessly drunk.
> Moreover I stay drunk, no matter what
>   I do to become sober.
> Rana, who disapproves, gave me one basket
>   with a snake in it.
> Mira folded the snake around her neck, it
>   was a lover's bracelet, lovely!
> Rana's next gift was poison: "This
>   is something for you, Mira."

She repeated the Holy Name in her chest,
     and drank it, it was good!
Every name He has is praise; that's
     the cup I like to drink, and
only that.
"The Great Dancer is my husband,"
Mira says, "rain washes off
     all the other colors."[16]

This poem describes what music did for me as a child. "The Great Dancer" of mystical consciousness "wash[ed] off all the other colors." Rana was Mira's brother-in-law. He really did send her a snake and poison, so outraged was her family by her nonconformity. It seems that she knew how not to be a victim of small-mindedness! "Mira folded the snake around her neck, it was a lover's bracelet, lovely!" Mull over her words and how powerfully she handles poison.

What I find interesting and empowering is that Mira is not a martyr; she uses the evil around her and turns it, through her ecstatic joy and play, into loveliness and goodness. Even an advanced martial artist would hope for this transmutation, taking someone's anger, hatred, and fear and flipping it into such obviousness that the negativism turns into bracelets, a drink, maybe a wake-up call to the perpetrator. Let us share one more poem:

> *Why Mira Can't Go Back to Her Old House*
> The colors of the Dark One have penetrated Mira's
>   body; all the other colors washed out.
> Making love with the Dark One and eating little,
>   Those are my pearls and my carnelians...
> ...Approve me or disapprove me: I praise the
>   Mountain Energy night and day.
> I take the path that ecstatic human beings
>   have taken for centuries.
> I don't steal money, I don't hit anyone.
>   What will you charge me with?

I have felt the swaying of the elephant's
    shoulders; and now you want me to
    climb on a jackass? Try to be serious.[17]

The Dark One, by the way, is Krishna, one of the pair of Divine Lovers. His partner in this image is Mira herself, her Self. In Hindu mythology and religion the divine is sexual; the altar consists of the *linga* and *yoni,* the male and female genitalia. Hinduism has always recognized the great power and pull and transformative heat that sexual imagery has on the human psyche and in the natural order. Many Hindu mystics are erotic, and most religious traditions also have this erotic mysticism, including John of the Cross, Teresa of Avila, Rumi, Kabir, and culturally different cosmogonic myths of creation.

Ecstasy: Understanding the Psychology of Joy

In his book, *Ecstasy: Understanding The Psychology of Joy,* Robert Johnson deals with the variegated forms of mystical bliss. Johnson, a Jungian analyst, is well known for his famous books on the psychological internal marriage in the trilogy, *She, He,* and *We.* Evidently a large portion of what occurs psychologically during ecstatic experiences is a merging, a unified functioning of the right and left hemispheres of the brain.

Music, which on every level is integrative, pulls us away from discord and brain hemispherical split into experiences of internal marriage. When I do meditation sessions on retreats, in workshops, or in my classes, I use music. I have found that no other medium works as quickly to help us enter our own centered place within. I do try in the Asian religion courses to keep the music the same as the culture we are studying as a way of adding to the enrichment of comprehending a culture from within. There is a lovely piece, for example, "Bamboo Flute," which is a solo Chinese rendition. Students calm down, watch their breathing, and enter the rounded garden gates of China through the music of that immense country.

I plan to attempt this same stratagem in my honors course on mysticism and add to the curriculum Robert Bly's book, *The Soul Is Here for Its Own Joy: Sacred Poems of Many Cultures.* The class will end its weekly three-hour evening session with a half-hour of reading aloud the poems of Kabir, Augustine, Dogen, Rilke, Mirabai, and others who dwell within that mystical home, the kingdom within.

I believe my own personal revelation from writing this chapter is how collaborative the mystical is for me. Icons remind me of significant poems, and the poems suggest certain musical selections. Each of these human forms express a felt state that makes the sacred tangible.

Transfigured Night

Arnold Schoenberg composed a multilayered piece entitled *Verklarte Nacht.* This work is romantically and erotically suggestive; for me it is one of the most moving musical works. When I was an undergraduate student in philosophy, I did an independent study on aesthetics focusing on the sculpture of Auguste Rodin. While in Paris, I took slides at the Musée Rodin, and upon my return to college in America, I gave a presentation of the slides to the accompaniment of *Verklarte Nacht.* The pathos of Rodin's works—the mixture of love, attraction, realness, such as in his famous statue, *The Kiss,* along with his works of raw suffering, illness, and war—were effectively viewed with Schoenberg's mystical music. I have shown that same presentation several times since, and always have the same reaction from the audience: a long, poignant silence.

Other musical works come to mind, works that are secular yet convey a sacred quality concerning human experience: for instance, among Ralph Vaughan Williams' works I especially love *The Lark Ascending,* to which I once did a liturgical dance. Samuel Barber's *Adagio for Strings,* which became one of America's favorite musical works, was chosen as the appropriate music to be played over the radio after the death of President Franklin Delano Roosevelt, and later after the death of President John F. Kennedy.

I must also include much of Beethoven, Brahms, Debussy, Prokofiev, and many, many more. These composers thought of themselves as secular. Bach, Rachmaninoff in his *Vespers,* Corelli, Byzantine chants for Christmas and Easter, and the works of Gregorian chant were specifically created with the sacred in mind. Bach has always been my favorite composer; as an adolescent I thought of this Lutheran giant and how he used to say that he wrote his music for God. Like the universe itself, I could always hear the oneness of the Divine melody below the layers of mathematical synchrony. One could almost discern a living breath, breathing rhythmically as the foundation of cosmic pattern and variety.

Om

In India the most sacred sound is *Om.* Om is the primordial sound reverberating from the Original Person, God, who as Divine Sperm and Womb created the universe. Om is the sound of the root mantra of all life. We know scientifically that an audio sound exists that is measurable through our twentieth-century radio instruments, and that scientists believe is a remnant chord of the Big Bang. In India when a baby goes through an entering rite into the family and community, her or his tongue is lightly touched with a toothpick dipped in gold signifying the golden sound of Om.[18]

When I have chanted Om, either alone in an Ashram, or with my students, I immediately discern physical changes taking place in my body. My breath becomes longer and deeper, centering in the belly, my voice becomes lower and much more relaxed, I can feel tense muscles loosening, and my mind becomes empty and free. Om is the root mantra pulsating in all our physiological functions, and as yogis have known for centuries, it is the key to body/mind/spirit integration. Om is the original musical sound that awakens our true nature back to reflecting on the truths, patterns, and balances within us and in the cosmos.

As I stated earlier in this chapter, I have always found in teaching meditation that music gets the class centered quickly. Our bodies and souls are patterned by music and function optimally with music. I also recommend studying to Bach or Mozart, for example, to relax and fully engage the mind. Biorhythmic training and the statistical study of people's retention of reading material while listening to certain composers have reaffirmed the validity of music's harmonious healing power.[19]

Plato and the Chinese philosophers believed that a world without music would fall apart. We know individually as well as socially that without the inspiration, harmony, and bodily soulfulness of musical rhythms, we become alienated from ourselves and other people. It is also significant to mention other life-forms from whom we become estranged. Paul Winter's music, for example, with wolves soulfully howling, whales lamenting, and solo flute and saxophone interrelating, intertwining, helps us get back to our soul as shared with other soulful creatures. In fact, there is music in nature itself: in the patterned rhythms of frogs croaking, birds singing, wind, rain, and in that healing silence during the quiet of winter.

Silent Music

I believe a book on mysticism would have to include the music of silence. Brother David Steindl-Rast wrote *The Music of Silence* as a companion to the best-selling Gregorian compact disc *Chant*. The subtitle of the book is *Entering the Sacred Space*, that space centered within what traditionally we have termed *soul*. In Brother David's words:

> The message...is to live daily with the *real* rhythms of the day. To live responsively, consciously, and intentionally, directing our lives from within, not being swept along by the demands of the clock, by external agendas, by mere reactions to whatever happens. By living in the real rhythms, we ourselves become more real. We learn to listen to the music of this moment, to hear its sweet implorings, its sober directives. We learn to dance in our hearts, to open our inner gates a crack more, to hearken to the music of silence, the divine life breath of the universe.[20]

Gregorian chants number about three thousand. It is believed that they probably originated from Jewish chants heard in Syria and Palestine. Pope Gregory I began preserving the chants in the late sixth and early seventh centuries.[21] Today we certainly witness a lay revival of interest in chant. From *Chant* by the Benedictine Monks of Santo Domingo de Silos to Hildegard of Bingen's *Canticles of Ecstasy*.

Gregorian chant is monophonic as are the chants of many other cultures, including Hindu, Buddhist, and Islamic. In Gregorian chant no musical instruments besides the human voice are employed, and chants are "sung in free rhythm."[22] This is not always true in Hindu and Muslim chanting, where musical instruments are often played improvisationally.

For a real Sufi experience, I recommend the *qawwali*
singing style of Pakistan's Sufi Muslim mystic Nusrat Fateh
Ali Khan, whose CDs and cassettes are readily available in
the United States. Even American fans regard him shamani-
cally as well as musically the best. Music has been his family's livelihood and love on both maternal and paternal sides
for over 600 years. A reviewer in the *New York Times* of one
of his concerts describes the experience:

> Each song began with a slow, quiet introductory sec-
> tion (or alap), a foreshadowing of the music to come.
> From there, a rhythmic pulse began on the table, a ref-
> erence point for the audience as Mr. Khan brought
> them into his web of vocal acrobatics and devotional
> lyrics. Most of these are Sufi poems renouncing the
> self and praising God with lines like, "Uniting with
> Him, I have drowned myself."

> Mr. Khan would slowly bring the music up to a fever
> pitch of ecstatically repeated phrases (each, like
> snowflakes, slightly different from the others) and then
> lower the intensity for a breather before taking the wail-
> ing music up to an even higher peak. Gesturing slowly
> and expansively with his hands, he seemed to be outlin-
> ing the shapes of the sounds he made as he conducted
> his improvising ensemble. When the music was at its
> best, the effect was catharsis. Pakistanis in the audience
> leaped out of their seats, dancing down the aisles to
> throw money at Mr. Khan. When asked what he does
> with this money, Mr. Khan said he gives it to charity or
> to singers who used to perform with his father.[23]

In terms of the songs, the reviewer states:

> Mr. Khan quoted a ghazal (or love song) and reflection
> on mortality that he recorded "Mera Piyya Ghar
> Aaya." "After a long wait, we have been united," the
> lyrics say of the singer and his beloved. "But even this

union is not to the liking of the clock, which is continuously striking the hour, mindless of how its sound makes my heart constrict. It is announcing that the hour of departure is drawing nearer. Someone, please, take this clock away."[24]

It is a great combination of ecstatic singing, instrumental proficiency, and pure electricity.

Body and Soul Becoming Centered

Chant is prayer and singing: musical praying. In Tibetan Buddhism, chanting is the mainstay of most ritual and worship. The rhythms of chant calm us, open us, and bring us into that sacred space where awe meets the divine soul to soul, center to center. Sometimes the rhythms, as in Mr. Kahn's chanting, are calming in a cathartic way, bringing us into a state of ecstatic aliveness. We at once awaken into a vibratory calm, intimately integrating our senses and our Spirit as the ocean, sex, or certain forms of art do.

We know from medical research that the endorphins in the brain are activated by arousing stimuli. These stimuli can then lead to healing and transformation. Sound stimuli that is calming, such as Gregorian chant or the sound of a heartbeat, may lead one to renewed health and new mental passageways. Dr. Jeanne Achterberg, in her book *Imagery in Healing: Shamanism and Modern Medicine,* speaks of the calming space created in the mind by heartbeat sounds:

> In a study with severely burned babies, I used sounds of a heart beat *[sic]* recorded in utero—similar in nature to drum beats—to create anesthesia. The heart sounds were capable of inducing sleep even during painful dressing changes. After the children became accustomed to the tape recorder in their cribs, they would fall asleep within minutes after it was turned on.[25]

Dr. Achterberg discusses at length the effects of chanting, drumming, and heartbeat as a shamanic path historically practiced as a way to the inner world and freedom. She speaks of realities such as pain being "gated or filtered out [so that] the mind would then be free to expand into other realms."[26]

The spiritual purpose of chant is centering. But more than getting to that sacred place interiorly, once we are there, chant, drums, ecstasy, are roads helping us to expand into other countries of the self. Each cultural expression may help us to center, and then, depending on a particular culture's religious emphasis, aid us to that place. For example, Christian and Buddhist compassion and peace, Muslim ecstasy and sensual appreciation, Hindu consciousness of the truth birthing bliss, nature's mythic sounds, or the heartbeat of a loved one bring us the gift of solidity and safety.

I have written this section with a seven-week-old puppy on my lap—he insisted on sleeping with me from his first day home. His three pounds contain a wealth of warmth, love, and solace. I am glad he feels rested and comforted by my heartbeat, I would like him to know how great a gift his soft breathing, extraordinary and ordinary mysticism, playful biting, and unconditional gaze of love mean to me. *Merci,* Wishbone.

Solitude and Art: Painting Practicum

Today there are numerous books and workshops on how to reconnect with the artist within ourselves. Associated with the right hemisphere of the brain, spirituality teaches of the qualities of artistry, trust, intuition, love, and imagination, symbolized frequently by the inner child archetype. Picasso once said, "We are all born artists. What do adults do to children to kill that spirit?"

Workshops are available on becoming more spiritually intuitive, on journaling, on learning to draw from the right brain, on gardening, liturgical dance, even chanting and drumming. The latter are especially popular among women's and men's groups trying to reestablish earth-based religious experiences. Chants and drumming are often performed in tents, yurts, or outside under the stars.

In a culture where adults are uncomfortable dancing unless they are at a wedding, and where the experience of music has become that of watching a performance rather than of being a part of the playing, people want to paint, dance, write, make music, and live in the spirit of spontaneity once again. People want the spontaneous spirit of the young child who loves his or her body and expressiveness and has not learned to turn away from that abandon and love through socially imposed inhibitions.

We have seen in this chapter the intricate union of spirituality and the arts expressed through different cultures. I will conclude this chapter by describing the eight years of solitude I had on sixty-five acres of evergreen trees surrounding a limpid lake.

The Classic Cabin in the Woods

My husband, Harry Smith, and I moved to Sussex County, New Jersey, near Delaware Water Gap to a cabin in the coniferous woods about fifteen years ago. We lived there for eight years, he working on his philosophical writing and learning the craft of carpentry, and I painting and giving workshops and retreats.

What I learned during those years has been foundational in my life: the lessons of quieting down, having minimal money and possessions, intuitively comprehending the language of the Spirit through nature (Bonaventure's book educating one on God's language revealed in nature and mirroring one's own mind), learning to value individuality and solitude. Finally, I developed an awareness that real growth takes place within and through one's vocation, helping the community in establishing spiritual and ethical priorities.

Painting Practicum

Lessons gained from that gifted time are in my paintings. I took the first three years to wrestle with style and form; the content was all around and within me. After those experimental years, I grew into a style that combined oil paints, acrylic paint, and metallic enamels in very organic forms.

In hindsight, I think it was spiritually meaningful that I began painting in mathematical patterns with realistic drawings of places, animals, and objects and evolved into the moving essence of the being or object in itself. For example, in the painting *Blood Dance,* I was attempting to convey the spiritual energy active in the material form called blood. Attempting to portray the life force of blood in its manifold functions, I wanted to show that within these functions, blood does dance. For instance, when we focus on healing an illness that is blood-related, it is imperative to center on the positive spiritual energy active in blood, especially if one is practicing a visualizing healing meditation. It is that essential healing energy that I was trying to convey on canvas.

Inner and Outer Space

The liberation of those years was, I realize now, awesome and rare. Moments of complete emptiness were coupled with a receptivity to how the universe works and to how a human being may express those workings in art and life. Once during a gentle snowfall, a great blue heron landed not thirty feet away from me on the lake's icy surface. I could distinctly hear the hum of her wings and was enraptured by the beauty of that many-hued white, gray, and blue moment.

The exhibitions of my paintings were entitled *Inner and Outer Space.* Several art critics cited the spirituality of the paintings as being a "womanly" view of reality. I was pleased with that type of recognition because I was trying to be true to myself through my own intuitions and intellectual reflections and by observing the natural world—often cited as a more right-brain, more womanly way of knowing.

Taoist Influences

I was also blessed by more and more immersion in Taoism. It was during those eight years that I truly became aware of synchronistic events, through avidly reading and utilizing the Chinese *I Ching: The Book of Change.* The first copy I ever bought was lying in the sun at a local flea market with a bright green and pink yin-yang symbol on its cover. A quarter was the price of this priceless treasure. When I brought the "Ching" home, I wrapped it in a piece of pink velvet cloth to demonstrate the reverence I recognized in that text's eternal wisdom.

My paintings *Mysterious Agreement* and *Zone Two* concern the sacred within microscopic, sky, water, and galactic realities. I was trying to express Taoist insights into the significance of yin (receptivity), with the yang of energetic forms. This is what the critics were calling "womanly," and one can see that labeling as correct since our culture is primarily still patriarchal and left-brain. I was attempting in my own spirituality to become yin and yang developmentally.

In a culture that is so yang, the balance of yin *with* yang was viewed as more yin!

Our culture is continuing the process of attempting to balance yin and yang as a paradigm for lifestyle and vocation. As previous chapters of this book suggest, the issues of education, child care, quality time for prayer/meditation, complementary medical treatment and healing, and creative leisure are slowly changing the workplace and home. The ways of spirituality and the arts will be recognized as more and more necessary as our culture becomes wholistically mature.

Putting It All Together

I was graced in those lakeside years by a partner whose philosophical nature and mind were compatible with mine. I also reread my old Thomas Merton books to help me through the agonies of introspection and found solace in the scientific research I was independently pursuing in astronomy, cosmology, and biology.

Harry would quote Bertrand Russell, who commented that his mathematics helped him gain detachment when life's problems became overwhelming. Harry, Merton, Taoistic truths alive in nature, and gorgeous photos of the Eagle nebulae and of blood samples helped me understand dimensions of my own inner world that were unnerving.

Surely one of the gifts of solitary artistry is that there are few avenues for distraction and escape. To be able to paint through my own therapeutic process; to paint the knowing wisdom arriving with the deepening awareness of the Spirit active in life's patterns; to paint feelings of beauty, suffering, and hope gave me a powerful ally within myself in the search for spiritual balance and harmony.

Christian Mysticism West and East

Much of the Christian mysticism in the West and East of my childhood began to bear fruit during our years in the woods. In a world that was quiet and simple, I learned to discern priorities and comprehend the voice of the Spirit through that prioritization. When I began my graduate studies in religion after those eight years of solitude, I knew which mystics rang true for me and which dogmas blocked the Way.

I try now to be "in the world, but not of it," to pass on to my son and to my students the spiritual-artistic gifts that religion at its best conveys.

A Global Perspective

In my life thus far I have learned tremendous lessons from the traditions of Taoism, Buddhism, Sufism, and Hinduism. Once while giving a workshop, "Stages of Spiritual Growth: A Global Perspective," I had everyone do a meditation visualizing our spiritual teachers. The image in my mind's eye was of Jesus in the lotus posture with eyes gently focused, surrounded by a circular rainbow, and with children from various ethnic backgrounds meditating with him. That vision is my global perspective in the hope of continually growing in relationship with God, staying in the alive rainbow of new insights, teaching and drawing forth in mutuality the child archetype within adults and children in my learning environmental community.

I hope to continue to learn and benefit from the teachings of diverse cultures for all the profound reasons of worldwide respect and understanding among peoples and, significantly in my personal journey as well, because such studies create joy and make of the spiritual journey a fascinating voyage into the presence of God revealed in inner and outer space. Bon voyage.

Notes

I. Finding the Center

1. William Johnston, trans., *The Cloud of Unknowing* (New York: Image Books, 1973), p. 7.
2. Jean Leclercq, O.S.B., *The Love of Learning and the Desire for God,* translated by C. Misrahi (New York: Fordham University Press, 1982), p. 263.
3. We know, for example, that he translated Denis the Areopagite's *Mystical Theology.*
4. Clifton Wolters, trans., *The Cloud of Unknowing* (New York: Penguin Books, 1978), p. 63.
5. *The Cloud* (trans. Wolters), p. 68.
6. *The Cloud* (trans. Johnston), p. 50.
7. Ibid., pp. 50–51.
8. Ibid., p. 100.
9. Ibid., p. 93.
10. *The Cloud* (trans. Wolters), p. 67.
11. Cf. Luke 10:39.
12. Cf. Elisabeth Schusler Fiorenza, *In Memory of Her* (New York: Crossroad, 1984), p. 330. There are many new and emerging books on the feminist reconstruction of what was distorted historically. I mention here only one: Elisabeth Moltmann-Wendel's *The Women Around Jesus* (New York: Crossroad, 1982), where entire chapters are devoted to Martha, Mary of Bethany, and Mary Magdalene.
13. *The Cloud* (trans. Johnston), p. 58.

14. Actually her full name, Kuan Shih Yin, means "she who hearkens to the cries of the world."

15. Cf: John Daido Loori's translation in *The Eight Gates of Zen* (Mt. Tremper, N.Y.: Dharma Communications, 1992), p. 243: "Sentient beings are numberless; I vow to save them."

16. *The Cloud* (trans. Wolters), pp. 63–64; cf. n. 7 for an emphasis on living in the present moment and the importance of how precious God's presence is if we allow for quality time commitments.

17. *The Cloud* (trans. Johnston), p. 83.

18. *The Cloud* (trans. Wolters), p. 43.

19. Paul Reps, ed., *Zen Flesh, Zen Bones: A Collection of Zen and Pre-Zen Writings* (New York: Doubleday, 1989), p. 114.

20. *The Cloud* (trans. Wolters), p. 146.

21. Ibid., p. 71.

22. Pema Chodron, *The Wisdom of No Escape and the Path of Loving-Kindness* (London: Shambala, 1991), pp. 76–77.

23. 1 Thes 5:17.

24. Irénée Hausherr, *The Name of Jesus,* trans. C. Cummings (Kalamazoo, Mich.: Cistercian Publications, 1978), p. 288.

25. Ibid., quoting N. Cranic's *Das Jesusgebet*, p. iv.

26. Ibid., pp. v–iv.

27. *The Cloud* (trans. Wolters), p. 69.

28. Ibid.

29. G. E. H. Palmer, P. Sherrard, and Kallistos Ware, *The Philokolia*, Vol. I (London: Faber and Faber, 1984), from St. Hesychios, p. 190.

30. From Diadochus of Photice arose the emphasis on the *Glykytes* (sweetness of God). For example, see chapter 61, "On Spiritual Knowledge," I. Hausherr's translation in *The Name of Jesus*, p. 85:

    Since we are babies when it comes to the art of perfect

> prayer, we absolutely have to have the help of the
> Spirit, so that all our concepts and thoughts may be
> penetrated and sweetened by the effect of [God's]
> wondrous sweetness.

Others have practiced *Iesou glykytate* as the wonderful mantra "Sweet Jesus."

31. *The Philokolia,* Vol. II (London: Faber and Faber, 1986), from St. Maximos the Confessor, p. 63.

32. Writings and biographies on Augustine abound with elaborations on his balanced theological approach. For example, Peter Brown, in his biography, *Augustine of Hippo* (Los Angeles: University of California, 1967), p. 28, states that Augustine's *Confessions* have to do with a journey of the heart; and Oliver O'Donovan, in *The Problem of Self-Love in Saint Augustine* (New Haven: Yale University Press, 1980), p. 116, states that Augustine is an affective intellectual.

    In Augustine's own writings, see, for example, *Homilies on the Gospel of John* in *The Nicene and Post-Nicene Fathers*, ed. Philip Schaff (Grand Rapids, Mich.: Eerdmans, 1956); *Tractate* LV:8, p. 299: "[God] has awakened in us a great longing for the sweet experience of [God's] presence within." In the *Expositions on the Book of Psalms*, in *The Nicene and Post-Nicene Fathers,* ed. A. C. Coxe (Grand Rapids, Mich.: Eerdmans, 1956); *Psalm* VI:9, p. 19: "...the soul's space is her affection."

33. Mahatma Gandhi, *All Men Are Brothers* (New York: Columbia University Press, 1958), p. 62. See also page 73:

> Meetings and group organizations are alright. They
> are like the scaffolding that an architect erects—a
> temporary and makeshift expedient. The thing that
> really matters is an invisible faith that cannot be
> quenched.

II. Becoming Whole: Finding Light, Discovering Peace

1. *Byzantine Theology: Historical Trends and Doctrinal Themes* (New York: Fordham University Press, 1983), p. 75.
2. Symeon the New Theologian, *The Discourses,* translated by C. J. de Catanzaro (New York: Paulist Press, 1980), IV: 445–50, p. 82.
3. Cf. also Psalm 18:6:

> In my distress I called upon the Lord;
>> to my God I cried for help.
> From his temple he heard my voice,
>> and my cry to him reached his ears.

Psalm 30:5:

> Weeping may tarry for the night,
>> but joy comes in the morning.

Psalm 42:3:

> My tears have been my food
>> day and night.

4. See, for example, Lk 7:38, 7:44; Jn 11:35; Acts 20:9, 20:31; 2 Cor 2:4; 2 Tim 1:3; Heb 5:7; 12:17; Rev 7:17; 21:4.
5. English translation by Dr. Sebastian Brock, Niewe Reeks, Deel XXIII, No. 1 (Wiesbaden, 1969), p. 252. For more primary sources on Isaac, see also *The Ascetical Homilies of Saint Isaac The Syrian,* translated by Holy Transfiguration Monastery (Boston, 1984).
6. *John Climacus,* translated by Colin Luibheld and Norman Russell (New York: Paulist Press, 1982), p. 141.
7. Psalms 42:1–4; 43–3. See also Albert Gelin's *The Psalms Are Our Prayers*, translated by Michael J. Bell (Collegeville, Minn.: Liturgical Press, 1964).
8. Symeon, *Discourses*, XX:73, p. 233.
9. Meyendorff, *Byzantine Theology*, p. 74.

10. Translated by Asheleigh Moorhouse (New York: St. Vladimir's Seminary Press, 1983), p. 144.
11. Quoted in Basil Krivocheine, *In the Light of Christ: Saint Symeon the New Theologian,* translated by Anthony Gythiel (New York: St. Vladimir's Seminary Press, 1986), p. 237.
12. Ibid., quoting Symeon in *Action de grâces* II: 82–89, pp. 383–84.
13. *Discourses,* VIII:28–29, p. 144.
14. Ibid., XX:209–215, p. 237.
15. Symeon, *Ethical Discourse* 4:424–429, quoted in Krivocheine's discourse, *In the Light,* pp. 200–201.
16. I have taken the liberty in certain instances of incorporating inclusive language. Most of the authors in this book are pre-1970s American. Therefore, I have when possible altered the "man's" to "humans," and have accorded as many "she's" and "her's" as "his" and "him's" in my own text.
17. Krivocheine, *In the Light,* quoting Symeon from *Ethical Discourses* II:167–86, p. 205.
18. Lossky, *The Vision,* pp. 161–62.
19. Krivocheine, *In the Light,* quoting from *Action de grâces,* l:152–154, p. 206.
20. Lossky, *The Vision,* p. 161.
21. It is significant to note that Symeon wrote the *Hymns* later in life at the apex of his own mystical development. Much more liberated and free from the worries of his earlier moralistic reforms, Symeon now soared in these paeans of the *Unio Mystica.* Symeon, *In the Light, Hymn,* 39:56–66, p. 233.
22. Ibid, *Hymn* 34:103–107, p. 233.
23. Symeon, *Discourses,* XXI:156, p. 242.
24. (Boston: Shambhala, 1994), p. 101.

25. *Hymns of Divine Love,* translated by George A. Maloney, S.J. (Danville, N.J.: Dimension Books, 1975), *Hymn 43,* p. 225.
26. Ibid., *Hymn 58,* p. 296.
27. Symeon, *The Discourses,* IV:71–719, p. 89.
28. Lossky, *The Vision,* pp. 145–146.
29. Ibid., pp. 41–42.
30. Syméon, *In the Light, Catéchèses* 22:165–168, p. 216.
31. Symeon, *Hymns, Hymn 1,* 38–40, p. 235.
32. Syméon Le Nouveau Théologien, *Catéchèses,* translated by Joseph Paramelle, S.J. Introduction and textual notes by Archbishop Basile Krivocheine, Vol. II (Paris: Sources Chrétiennes, 1964); *Catéchèse* XV:69–71, p. 227. All the English from French translations here and below are mine.
33. (New York: New American Library, 1974), p. 177.
34. (Kalamazoo, Mich.: Cistercian Publications, 1986), p. 332.
35. Krivocheine, *In the Light, Hymn 30:* 467–472; *Hymn 30,* 474–487; *Hymn 36:* 58–62, p. 387.
36. Symeon, *Hymns, Hymn 43,* p. 222.
37. Symeon, *Discourses,* XXII:19, p. 243.
38. Symeon *In the Light, Ethical Chapters,* 6:137–178, p. 289.
39. Syméon Le Nouveau Théologien, *Traités Théologiques et Éthiques,* translated by Jean Darrouzés, Vol. I: *Théologiques* III:144–160 (Paris: Sources Chrétiennes, 1966), p. 165.
40. Nicétas Stéthatos, *Un Grand Mystique Byzantine: Vie de Syméon Le Nouveau Théologien,* translated by Irénée Hausherr, S.J. (Rome: Orientalia Christiana, 1928). *Vie* 113–124.
41. Ibid., *Vie,* 119–122. See also Archbishop Krovocheine's *In the Light of Christ,* esp. p. 59; Ewert H. Cousins; *A Blueprint for a Cross-Cultural Study of Mysticism,* Vol. 17 (Madras: Radhakrishnan Institute, 1985), p. 19: "Mys-

tics, by participating in God's self-communicating energy, become themselves self-diffusive: in teaching, writing, preaching, guiding others, or in administering and organization."

42. Diane Dreher, *The Tao of Inner Peace* (New York: Harper-Collins, 1990), p. xiii.

43. *Tao Te Ching,* translated by Gia-Fu Feng and Jane English (New York: Vintage, 1972), N.P., Section One.

44. Ibid., Section Six.

45. *The I Ching* or *Book of Changes*, the Richard Wilhelm translation rendered in English by Cary F. Baynes (Princeton: Princeton University Press, 1977), p. xxxv.

46. Symeon, *Hymns, Hymns 23,* p. 118.

47. Symeon, *The Discourses*, II:251, p. 53.

48. *Catherine of Siena* (Hyde Park, N.Y.: New City Press, 1993), p. 15.

49. Ibid.

50. *Catherine of Siena*, translated by Suzanne Noffke, O.P., *The Dialogue* (New York: Paulist Press, 1980), *Tears,* p. 161.

51. Raimondo da Capua, *Legenda Major,* translated by C. Kearns, *The Life of Catherine of Siena* (Wilmington, Del.: Michael Glazier, 1980), *Life*, II:1, p. 121.

52. Catherine, *The Dialogue*, p. 169.

53. Ibid., p. 175.

54. Ibid., compare, for example, p. 171.

55. Dreher, *The Tao of Inner Peace,* bases her quotation on Lin Yutang's *The Wisdom of Laotse:* "The people of the world are brought into a community of heart/and the sage regards them all as his children" (p. 231).

56. Catherine of Siena, *The Letters*, Vol. I, translated by Suzanne Noffke, O.P. (Binghamton, N.Y.: State University of New York, 1988), *Letter 73*, p. 227.

57. Ibid., *Letter 76,* to Pope Gregory XI in Avignon, p. 234.
58. F. C. Happold, *Mysticism: A Study and Anthology* (London: Penguin Books, 1990), p. 101.
59. Catherine, *The Letters, Letter 76,* p. 235.
60. Ibid., *Letter 88,* p. 266.
61. Catherine, *The Dialogue,* p. 171.
62. Thich Nhat Hanh, *Peace is Every Step,* from the foreword by His Holiness the Dalai Lama (New York: Bantam, 1991), n.p.
63. Noffke, Introduction, in Catherine, *The Dialogue,* p. 9.
64. Catherine, *Letters,* Noffke's comment on *Letter 60,* p. 33, n. 14.
65. Alois Maria Haas, "Schools of Late Medieval Mysticism," in *Christian Spirituality: High Middle Ages and Reformation,* p. 167, edited by Jill Raitt (New York: Crossroad, 1987).
66. Noffke, *Introduction,* in Catherine, *The Dialogue,* p. 4.
67. Swami Abhishiktananda (Dom Henri le Saux), *Saccidananda: A Christian Approach to Advaitic Experience* (New Delhi: I.S.P.C.K., 1984), p. 176.
68. Ibid., p. 177.
69. Ibid., p. 176.
70. Juan Mascaro, trans., *The Bhagavad Gita* (New York: Penguin, 1982), 2:38, p. 51.
71. Gene Sharp, "Nonviolent Sruggle: An Effective Alternative," in *Inner Peace, World Peace: Essays on Buddhism and Nonviolence,* edited by Kenneth Kraft (New York: State University of New York, 1992), p. 116.
72. Ibid., p. 122. For a diverse selection of readings, including religious writers and texts, and a more extensive list of Sharp's alternatives to violence, "198 Methods of Nonviolent Action," see also *A Peace Reader: Essential Readings on War, Justice, Non-Violence, and World Order,* edited by J. Fahey and R. Armstrong (New York: Paulist Press, 1992).

73. Ibid., p. 123. Or as Mahatma Gandhi put it, "I do believe that the most spiritual act is the most practical in the true sense of the term" (chap. 2, n. 40).
74. David Kinsley, *Hinduism: A Cultural Perspective* (Englewood Cliffs, N.J.: Prentice Hall, 1993), p. 24.
75. *The Bhagavad Gita,* trans. Mascaro, 3:7, p. 56.
76. *Chuang Tzu: Basic Writings,* trans. Burton Watson (New York: Columbia University Press, 1996), p. 70.
77. From Jane Hirschfield, *Women in Praise of the Sacred: 43 Centuries of Spiritual Poetry by Women* (New York: HarperPerennial, 1995), p. 163.

III. The Divine Within

1. See Annemarie Schimmel's extensive references to al-Hallaj in *Mystical Dimensions of Islam* (Chapel Hill: University of North Carolina Press, 1975).
2. See, for example, from as early as Rudolf Otto's *Mysticism East and West: A Comparative Analysis of the Nature of Mysticism* (New York: Macmillan, 1932), to Bernard McGinn's many publications on Meister Eckhart pertaining to interreligious dialogue.

   The interreligious newsletter published through Osage Benedictine Monastery (Rt. 1, Box 3842, Sand Springs, OK 74063) contains the latest information on contemplative publications and retreats worldwide. It usually also contains at least one article on interreligious subjects of interest.
3. There is ample psychological evidence on this topic of *transference* in both the Freudian and Jungian literature.
4. Anthony deMello was a Jesuit from Bombay, India. Especially pertinent to our studies here is his *Sadhana: A Way to God, Christian Exercises in Eastern Form,* which may be purchased through the Institute for Jesuit

Sources, Fusz Memorial, St. Louis University, St. Louis, MO 63108.

5. The Ashram publishes an extensive catalog on interreligious books, global awareness, and international music. (Yogaville, VA 23921).

6. "Commentary on the Book of Exodus," N. 16. LW II, p. 22, 3–6. This translation is Reiner Schurmann's in his profound book *Meister Eckhart: Mystic and Philosopher* (Bloomington: Indiana University Press, 1978), p. 120.

7. Ibid., see p. 247, n. 140.

8. From the Foreword to *Meister Eckhart: The Essential Sermons, Commentaries, Treatsies, and Defense,* translated by Edmund Colledge and Bernard McGinn (New York: Paulist Press, 1981), p. xvii.

9. Ibid., *Theological Summary,* p. 24.

10. Quoted in Jill Raitt, ed., *Christian Spirituality: High Middle Ages and Reformation,* Vol. 17 of *World Spirituality: An Encyclopedic History of the Religious Quest* (New York: Crossroad, 1987), p. 28.

11. Quoted from *Commentary on the Book of Wisdom* #154, in *Meister Eckhart: Teacher and Preacher,* edited by Bernard McGinn (New York: Paulist Press, 1987), p. 169.

12. Paul Reps, ed., *Zen Flesh, Zen Bones* (London: Doubleday, 1989), p. 115.

13. Thomas Cleary and J. C. Cleary, eds., *The Blue Cliff Record* (London: Shambhala, 1992).

14. Erich Fromm, D. T. Suzuki, and Richard DeMartino, *Zen Buddhism and Psychoanalysis* (London: Harper Colophon Books, 1960).

15. Ibid., p. 19.

16. *Commentary on John,* n. 562, quoted in Colledge and McGinn, *Meister Eckhart,* p. 35.

17. Lucien Stryk and Takashi Ikemoto, eds. and trans., *Zen Poetry* (London: Penguin Books, 1981), p. 68.

18. Schurmann's translation in *Meister Eckhart: Mystic and*

Philosopher: "Gotes sin min sin und gotes isticheit min isticheit." From the sermon "Justi vivent in aeternum" (see pp. 87 and 240).

19. Ashley Montagu, *Growing Young* (Granby, Mass.: Bergin and Garvey, 1989), p. 95.

20. Ibid., p. 134.

21. Ibid., p. 175.

22. "Too much of our learning is done without thought, and such learning is labor lost. Our schools are severely to blame here, for there is little or no education in them. What passes for education is largely instruction, training in the skills and techniques of the three 'R's.' Too often education consists in teaching children what to think, rather than *how* to think. We don't give children problems to solve, we give them answers to remember" (ibid., p. 116).

    "And what is imagination really? It is play—playing with ideas. As the child replied when she was asked what she did when she made a drawing, 'First I think, and then I draw a line round my think'" (ibid., p. 132).

23. In Halcyon Backhouse, *The Best of Meister Eckhart* (New York: Crossroad, 1995), p. 15.

24. Ibid.

25. Ibid., p. 13.

26. Evelyn Underhill, *Mysticism* (New York: New American Library, 1974), p. 118.

27. Ibid., p. 122.

28. *The Best of Meister Eckhart,* p. 35.

29. Stryk and Ikemoto, eds., *Zen Poetry,* p. 146.

30. Gregory Palamas, *The Triads,* transcribed by Nicholas Gendle (New York: Paulist Press, 1983), *The Uncreated Glory,* p. 89. Cf., Grégoire Palamas, *Défense Des Saints Hésychastes* (Louvain: Université Catholique, 1959). Triad III, 3, 10, pp. 712–714: "Ne vois-tu pas que les

hommes unis à Dieu et déifiés, qui fixent divinement leurs regards sur lui, ne voient pas commes nous?"

31. Ibid., *Deification in Christ*, p. 57.
32. Ibid.
33. *The Best of Meister Eckhart*, p. 14.
34. Abhishiktananda, *Prayer* (New Delhi: I.S.P.C.K., 1979).
35. Ibid., p. 25.
36. Ibid., p. 6.
37. Palamas, *The Triads, The Hesychast Method of Prayer* and *The Transformation of the Body*, I.ii.4, p. 43.
38. Miranda Shaw, *Passionate Enlightenment* (Princeton: Princeton University Press, 1994), pp. 26–27.
39. Amnesty International Annual Reports since the 1980s.
40. Robert Thurman, *Essential Tibetan Buddhism* (New York: HarperSanFrancisco, 1995), pp. 48–59.

IV. In the Image and Likeness of God

1. From Thich Nhat Hahn's video *Touching Peace*, produced by Legacy Media, Inc., Berkeley, Calif., 1993.
2. Matthew 6:29.
3. Kallistos Ware, *Ways of Prayer and Contemplation, Part I, Eastern* in *Christian Spirituality: Origins to the Twelfth Century*, edited by Bernard McGinn, John Meyendorff, and Jean Leclercq (New York: Crossroad, 1987), p. 412.
4. *Bonaventure*, translated by Ewert Cousins (New York: Paulist Press, 1978); *The Soul's Journey into God*, chapter 2, p. 78.
5. Ibid., p. 77.
6. Gregory wrote a biography, *The Life of Saint Macrina*, about his sister, portraying her spirituality and deeds as a model of saintliness. See *Saint Gregory of Nyssa: Asceti-*

cal Works, translated by Virginia Callahan (Washington, D.C.: Catholic University of America Press, 1967).

7. Gregory of Nyssa, *The Life of Moses*, translated by A. Malherbe and E. Ferguson (New York: Paulist Press, 1978), p. 3. See *The Life of Moses*, Book I:19 for reference.

8. Ibid., Book I:20, p. 34.

9. See Joseph Campbell, *The Hero with a Thousand Faces* (Princeton: Princeton University Press, 1973), esp. pp. 30–40.

10. *The Life of Moses*, Book I:19–20, pp. 34, 35; emphasis mine.

11. Ibid., Book I:20, p. 35.

12. Campbell, *The Hero*, p. 36.

13. *The Life of Moses*, Book II:227, 231, 232, pp. 113–115.

14. See *Two Zen Classics: Mumonkan and Hekiganroku*, translated by Katsuki Sekida (Tokyo: Weatherhill, 1977). Pages 250–251 explain gradual and sudden *satori* (realization) from a typically Zen perspective.

15. Gregory of Nyssa, *Commentary on the Song of Songs*, translated by Casimir McCambley (Brookline, Mass.: Hellenic College Press, 1987), Twelfth Homily, p. 213.

16. *Apophatic* theology is based on negating attributes or descriptions of the divine, as opposed to *cataphatic* theology, which affirms attributes or descriptions of God. Bernard McGinn, in *The Foundations of Mysticism* (New York: Crossroad, 1992), says, "Gregory created the first systematic negative theology in Christian history....All the main lines of Gregory's mystical thought—his understanding of the spiritual senses, his treatment of the stages of the soul's itinerary, as well as his teaching on the perception of the divine presence, on ecstasy, on the nature and kinds of contemplation, on divinization, and on union—are affected by this profound apophaticism" (pp. 41–42).

17. See Mircea Eliade, *The Sacred and the Profane*, translated by Willard Trask (New York: Harcourt Brace Jovanovich, 1959).

18. Song of Songs, Fifteenth Homily, p. 263.

19. Ibid., Third Homily, p. 84.

20. Ibid., First Homily, p. 55.

21. Vladimir Lossky, *In the Image and Likeness of God* (New York: St. Vladimir's Seminary Press, 1985), p. 37.

22. Charlene Spretnak in *States of Grace: The Recovery of Meaning in the Postmodern Age* (New York: Harper-Collins, 1991) elaborates on the contemporary loss of religious meaning. She rightly describes the more recent phenomenon of frantic consumerism as one of the worst developments in socially acceptable overkill in terms of "you are what you buy": "Our ontological range of possibilities may continue to shrink as marketing manipulation increases and our authentic sense of relatedness...decreases" (p. 3).

23. From the Introduction, Song of Songs, p. 24.

24. Song of Songs, Eleventh Homily, p. 203.

25. *Life of Moses*, I:46, p. 43.

26. Song of Songs, First Homily, p. 48.

27. Bede Griffiths, *The Marriage of East and West* (Springfield, Ill.: Templegate, 1982), p. 16.

28. Ibid., p. 113.

29. *The Upanishads*, translated by Swami Prabhavananda and F. Manchester (New York: New American Library, 1948), *Brihadaranyaka Upanishad*, p. 89.

30. Song of Songs, Tenth Homily, p. 195.

31. Raimundo Panikkar, *The Vedic Experience: Mantramanjari* (Berkeley: University of California Press, 1977), *Katha Upanishad*, p. 565.

32. Prabhavananda translation, p. 18.

33. *The Vedic Experience*, *Chandogya Upanishad*, pp. 753–757.

34. Song of Songs, Ninth Homily, p. 175.
35. M. K. Gandhi, *Satyagraha* (Ahmedabad, India: Navajivan Publishing House, 1951), p. 109.
36. Ewert Cousins, Introduction, *Bonaventure*, p. 1.
37. Ibid., p. 2.
38. *Bonaventure*, p. 55.
39. *The I Ching*, translated by Richard Wilhelm, Foreword by C. G. Jung (Princeton, N.J.: Princeton University Press, 1980).
40. *Chronica XXIV generalium*, in *Analecta franciscana*, III, p. 324.
41. Ibid., p. 356.
42. Introduction, *Bonaventure*, p. 20.
43. *Bonaventure*, Prologue, pp. 56–57.
44. Ibid., *The Soul's Journey*, chap. 1, pp. 59–60.
45. Ibid., pp. 62–63.
46. Ibid., p. 63.
47. See, e.g., Andrew McLaughlin's *Regarding Nature: Industrialism and Deep Ecology* (Albany: State University of New York, 1993).
48. *Bioregionalism* is the most articulate movement today concerning the importance of humans identifying with their surroundings, their place. See, e.g., Kirkpatrick Sale, *Dwellers in the Land: The Bioregional Vision* (San Francisco: Sierra Club Books, 1985).
49. Bonaventure, *The Soul's Journey*, chap. 1, pp. 67–68.
50. Bonaventure, *The Soul's Journey*, chap. 2, p. 69; emphasis mine.
51. Ibid., p. 76.
52. Ibid., p. 77. Bonaventure is drawing here from Romans 1:20.
53. Ibid., p. 78.
54. Shundo Aoyama, *Zen Seeds: Reflections of a Female Priest*, translated by P. Bennage (Tokyo: Kosei Publishing Company, 1990), p. 23.

55. Bonaventure, *The Soul's Journey*, chapter 3, p. 79.
56. Ibid.
57. Ibid.
58. *Two Zen Classics*, p. 218.
59. L. Stryk and T. Ikemoto, trans., *Zen Poems of China and Japan* (New York: Grove Weidenfeld, 1973), p. 111.
60. Bonaventure, *The Soul's Journey*, chapter 4, p. 87.
61. Ibid., p. 91.
62. Ibid., p. 93.
63. Ibid., p. 87.
64. Bonaventure, *The Soul's Journey*, chapter 5, p. 98.
65. Ibid., quoting Alan of Lille, *Regulae Theologicae*, reg. 7.
66. Ibid., chapter 6, p. 107.
67. Ibid., p. 109.
68. *De civitate Dei*, VIII:4.
69. Panikkar, *The Vedic Experience*, verse 19, p. 744.
70. Bonaventure, *The Soul's Journey*, chapter 5, p. 97.
71. Ibid., chapter 7, p. 110.
72. Ibid., p. 113.
73. Ibid., p. 115; Bonaventure quoting Dionysius, *De mystica theologia I*, 1.
74. Ibid., p. 116.
75. For elaborations on connections among religion, nature, and the environment, see *This Sacred Earth*, edited by Roger S. Gottlieb (New York: Routledge, 1996).
76. Gregory of Nyssa, *The Life of Moses*, Book II:174, 179, pp. 98–99.
77. Ibid., Book II: 200, p. 106.
78. See Justin O'Brien's interesting article, "Awakening Spirit: The Jesus Prayer," on the theme of praying unceasingly. *Yoga International*, June/July 1997, Issue No. 36.

V. Spirituality and the Arts

1. Paulist Press, 1993.
2. David Goa, *Mantra: Hearing the Divine in India* (Edmondton, Alta.: Anima Books, 1991). Quotations are from the cassette that accompanies the text.
3. Mahmoud Zibawi, *The Icon: Its Meaning and History* (Collegeville, Minn.: Liturgical Press, 1993), p. 98.
4. Ibid., p. 150, quoting L. Ouspensky, *Theologie de L'Icone*, p. 437.
5. Ibid., p. 140, quoting Giacometti, interview given to D. Sylvester in 1964; translation from French, in *Dessins de Giacometti* (Galerie Claude Bernard, 1975).
6. Ibid., p. 150. Yves Bonnefoy, *Un Reve Fait à Mantoue* (Paris: Mercure de France, 1967), p. 10.
7. Ibid., p. 98.
8. Ibid., quoting Paul Evdokimov, *L' Art de l' Icone, théologie de la Beaute* (Paris: Desclée de Brouwer, 1972), p. 221. Evdokimov's *The Art of the Icon,* translated by Steven Bingham, is available in English from Torrance, Calif.: Oakwood Publications, 1990.
9. Parker Palmer has several books in print. I recommend *To Know As We Are Known: Education As a Spiritual Journey* (San Francisco: HarperCollins, 1993).
10. W. B. Yeats, *Sailing to Byzantium* (New York: Macmillan, 1989), p. 193.
11. A lovely book on Chinese painting that contains many of the origins of Japanese Buddhist art is *Empty and Full: The Language of Chinese Painting* by Francois Cheng (Boston: Shambhala, 1994). For example, "Chinese aesthetic thought always envisions the beautiful in its relationship with the true" (p. 2) and "[p]ainting that reaches toward a spiritual process" (p. 60).
12. Jelaluddin Rumi, *Rumi: We are Three*, translated by Coleman Barks (Putney, Vt.: Maypop, 1987).

13. Mirabai, *Mirabai: Versions,* translated from the Rajasthani by Robert Bly (Penland, N.C.: Squid Ink, n.d.).

14. Robert Bly, ed., *The Soul Is Here for Its Own Joy: Sacred Poems from Many Cultures* (Hopewell, N.J.: Ecco Press, 1995), p. 183.

15. Ibid., p. 202.

16. *Mirabai: Versions.*

17. Ibid.

18. See Wendy Doniger O' Flaherty, *Hindu Myths* (London: Penguin Books, 1975).

19. On the technical research of biofeedback, see K. R. Gaarder and P. Montgomery, *Clinical Biofeedback: A Procedural Manual*; B. Brown, *New Mind, New Body*; D. S. Olton and A. R. Noonberg, *Biofeedback: Clinical Applications in Behavioral Medicine.*

20. David Steindl-Rast, O.S.B., *The Music of Silence* (Harper-SanFrancisco, 1994), p. 122.

21. Ibid., p. 2. For historical contextual information, see Joseph H. Lynch's *The Medieval Church* (London: Longman, 1992).

22. Ibid.

23. Neil Strauss, "Enchanter at the Crossroads of Pop and Sacred," *New York Times,* 18 August 1996, pp. 53 and 56. See also Jon Pareles, "Songs of Divine Love Convey Earthly Exuberance," *New York Times,* 23 August 1996, C2.

24. Ibid.

25. Jeanne Achterberg, *Imagery in Healing: Shamanism and Modern Medicine* (London: Shambhala, 1985), p. 43.

26. Ibid. See also A. Neher, "Auditory Driving Observed with Scalp Electrodes in Normal Subjects," *EEG and Clinical Neurophysiology* 13 (1961), pp. 449–451; A. Neher, "A Physiological Explanation of Unusual Behavior in Ceremonies Involving Drums," *Human Biology* 34

(1962), pp. 151–160. There is extensive research in this area. I recommend these articles and Dr. Achterberg's bibliography as a fine start.

Glossary

Ashram	In Hinduism, a community of living practitioners.
Bhagavad Gita	A part of the larger epic *Mahabharata,* describing the internal battle. Only two characters are in dialogue: the god Krishna, and the great warrior Arjuna.
Bhakti	In Hinduism, the path of devotional love.
Bodhisattva	Wisdom being. About to be a Buddha and freed into liberation, the Bodhisattva turns back to help teach the world about enlightenment. Embodiment of compassion.
Ch'an masters	Meditational school of Buddhism in China influenced by Taoist thought; traveled to Japan, influencing the development of Zen Buddhism.
Dharma	Truth, righteousness. In Hinduism and Buddhism, the moral reality of the universe also to be reflected in human behavior.
Eros	From the Greek "to love, to desire."
Hesychasm	From the Greek *hesychia,* "tranquility."

Hsin	Heart-mind. Chinese character symbolizing humane development.
Jnana	In Hindu tradition, the rarest path of wisdom and knowledge.
Kabbalah	Literally "tradition" in the Hebrew. The Jewish mystical tradition in its multifarious geographic and cultural post-biblical forms.
Kalachakra	"Wheel of time." A specific sand mandala in the Tibetan Buddhist tradition.
Karma	In Hindu and Buddhist philosophy, the law of cause and effect. Consequences ensue according to one's intentions and actions.
Karma Yoga	The path of good deeds. In Hinduism, to act according to dharma, not seeking the fruits of action. To act because one knows that is the "right" path, no matter the consequences. Gandhi's foundation for civil disobedience.
Koan	Ch'an or Zen conundrum used in meditation to clarify consciousness from the chattering of the false ego.
Mandala	From the sanskrit, "circle." Tantric painting mirroring the symbolic harmony of the mind and cosmos.
Newtonian physics	Scientific interpretation of reality based on the theories of Sir Isaac Newton. Pertaining specifically to

commonsense observation of the laws of gravitation and cause and effect results.

Nirvana   Literally "snuffing out" the fires of desire. Liberation from the cycles of karma and rebirth.

Penthos   Compunction. In the desert and patristic traditions, the rapid path of mourning and tears to purify our faults.

Quantum physics   Begun with Albert Einstein's theory of relativity. One emphasis is that all of reality is a web of interrelations including the observer.

Samsara   The suffering of the world. The recycling karma of existence.

Satchitananda   In Sanskrit, sat=truth, chit=consciousness, ananda=bliss. Considered the Hindu trinity embodying God-like awareness.

Suchness   The ability to be in the "eternal now." Experiencing existence "such as it is" through emptiness without the false ego's impositions.

Sunyata   Emptiness. In Mahayana Buddhism, all reality is foundationally empty; therefore, we must learn to quiet the mind through meditational practice in order to be receptive to that contemplative and cosmic reality.

Tantric	In Hindu and Buddhist tradition, certain schools emphasizing sexual symbolism leading the practitioner into internal states of mystical union and liberation.
Tao	In the Chinese religious tradition of Taoism, the Tao is literally translated as the "Way." Figuratively translated as the Source of all life reflected in the patterns of microcosmic and macrocosmic reality.
Upanishads	Literally the "secret teachings." Metaphysical instructions of classical Hinduism on the reality of the immortal Self.
Vedas	Beginning as oral tradition, the earliest and largest body of classical Hindu scriptures consisting of the Samhitas, Brahmanas, Aranyakas, and Upanishads.
Yin and Yang	Symbols of the complementarity of opposites that together manifest the Tao. Yin is the passive, yang the aggressive.

Index